AN INTRODUCTION TO
TECHNICAL DIVING

by Rob Palmer

UNDERWATER WORLD PUBLICATIONS

© Copyright 1994
by Underwater World Publications Ltd.
55 High Street, Teddington, Middlesex, TW11 8HA

First printed 1994

Reprinted 1995

Revised 1997

Front cover photograph by Leo Dickinson

Photography by Wes Skiles (p.102); Leo Dickinson (p.35, right); Gavin Newman (p.107); John Bantin (p.35, left; p.36); Stuart Clough (back cover); Rob Parker (p.103, right); John Selby (p.106).

All other photography by Rob Palmer

Line illustrations by Rico

Book edited by Mike Busuttili,
designed and produced by DIVER Magazine,
and printed by Emirates Printing Press,
PO Box 5106, Airport Road, Dubai, UAE

ISBN 0 946020 23 X

Acknowledgements

Over my diving career, there have been many individuals who have helped me develop my skills and to whom I am eternally grateful. For their indirect help throughout that time in producing this book, I would like to risk offending others by singling out, in alphabetical order to avoid any hint of favouritism, the late George Benjamin, John Bevan, Stuart Clough, the late Sheck Exley, Martyn Farr, Bret Gilliam, Bill Hamilton, Tom Mount, Sir John Rawlins, the late Oliver Statham, Wes Skiles, Bill Stone, Robin Turner, Mike Wooding, and Geoff Yeadon, for a mixture of guidance, direction and example in how things can be done if you try hard enough.

This book is dedicated to my father.
I wish he could have been here
to see me write it.

Rob Palmer

Contents

INTRODUCTION

Are the risks too great?

"If you are thinking one year ahead, plant rice.
If you are thinking ten years ahead, plant trees.
But if you are thinking one hundred years ahead, educate the people".

Old Chinese Proverb.

IS DIVING dangerous? When divers are well trained and they are diving within their technical limits, the answer should be "No". But every time the frontiers are pushed back these very concepts of completeness of training, and the establishment of limits must be called into question. Many dives which are considered acceptable today would have been classed as unnecessarily dangerous 10 years ago, and perhaps completely impossible 20 years ago. What was dangerous, or safe, in those days reflected the state of the world then. Time changes many things.

What makes diving dangerous? For a start, it is an activity that takes place where you can't breathe the atmosphere, so it is to a degree equipment-dependent, a technological sport, so the diver needs to thoroughly understand his or her equipment. Diving demands a degree of environmental awareness, and of the physical effect of the environment on the diver. It requires a basic knowledge of a few physical laws (Boyle's, Dalton's, etc) and a small degree of mathematical ability is required for the understanding of decompression procedures and gas consumption. This may sound a lot, but the knowledge required for simple, safe diving is simplicity itself. You need only to understand and accept the limits of your knowledge and ability, and that you must keep within those limits.

Diving is like several other "environmentally-committing" sports, such as yachting, mountaineering, caving or various forms of mannned flight. All of these activities have regard for wind, weather and exposure, they offer mounting degrees of complexity and difficulty as you progress upwards through the experience grades, and all of them offer you the ability to choose a level of activity and to stay there, happy that you are enjoying yourself within your limits. It is perfectly acceptable to aspire to perform an activity to the best of your ability, not necessarily in a competitive way, but within the higher levels of experience and performance that still sit happily in a recreational court. People still play hard for fun. It's a basic human need.

The major concern of most diving organisations has traditionally been to assure the beginner a safe and structured passage through the early days of their diving career. Their concern for safety has made diving safer than skiing, horse-riding, hockey, fishing, swimming and a host of other recreational activities. More people die while engaged in these activities than while diving.

This concern for the safety of the beginner has perhaps been at the expense of people at the upper end of the sport, who wish to continue learning and advancing their own skills safely to a higher degree. These divers are often very safety conscious indeed, and have abilities far beyond those of the average diver. Unfortunately, instead of being respected for what they wish to do, these people have traditionally been criticised for doing things that are considered far too dangerous. Try that one in a mountaineering or yachting club and see how far you get. There are those who criticise climbers who strive to ascend hard routes, or yachtsmen who sail around the world, and their view has every right to be heard, but they do not make the rules, and they are not allowed to limit the sport.

Let's make some arbitrary comparisons with a sport I grew up in – mountaineering. Most recreational diving activity takes place in relatively good weather and water conditions, to depths of about 40 metres. I'd see that as the equivalent of a good hill-walk on a spring or autumn day, when the weather might change and liven things up, but when most conditions can be anticipated. Or a low grade rock climb, where there is some exposure and difficulty, but where you are unlikely to fall off. The degrees of danger and exposure are about the same. The fact that things can go wrong more quickly underwater is set against the longer exposure to adverse conditions possible on an isolated hill – a dive is over in an hour or so, the walk or climb may take all day.

Standard recreational diving stops at the mountaineering equivalent of a simple winter climb, or at medium grade rock-climbing. The traditional training structure is not intended, nor especially suited, to go beyond this level. You are left either to learn by experience, or to try it anyway. If you dive deeper than 40 or 50 metres, if you change your gas mixtures, or dive inside something, you're taking yourself farther and farther outside the system. By the time you're doing the equivalent of a Grade 5 ice climb, or a E2 rock climb (both pretty standard and very well respected grades in mountaineering), you have left behind the limits of normal recreational diving.

How has this come about? Do the *real* dangers in diving lie in the reluctance to accept the potential for developing safer equipment, safer techniques, safer gas mixtures? Divers need to have advanced training that covers diving practices as well as boat handling, radio operation and navigational techniques. The latter are useful additional skills, not diving skills, and as such are perhaps not advanced diver training.

Part of the problem may simply be that some of the larger training organisations have got too big, and become too slow in their ability to respond to real changes in equipment, in technique, and in attitude. It usually takes about five years for a new skill or major equipment development to be accepted. In some cases, that's no bad thing: it gives time for it to be established in use, and for lessons to be learned. But, during this period, care should be taken not to criticise others for using such equipment or techniques. It is those at the technical sharp end who will be honing these techniques, developing the specialised equipment, and creating the new infrastructure for training.

There are ways to get you to places, responsibly, that you are not currently being trained to get to. But will you be prepared to learn again, to perhaps be more disciplined in your diving practice? Do you want more specialised training to be available that will make all your diving safer, shallow and deep, long and short? I hope so. But remember, even if the training is there, there is no compulsion to do it. While there will always be new places to explore, new limits to reach, there is no compulsion whatsoever to get there if you do not wish to go.

But all sports develop, and, by comparison with other activities, I don't believe diving is as dangerous as it is made out – *as long as proper training exists, and an acceptance of risk is there!* But while the boundaries are still placed where they currently are, much of the diving that is actually being done by advanced recreational divers will continue to be done outside the structure of recreational diving.

If mountaineering, caving, and all those other sports respect the people who push back the frontiers, why don't we? New boundaries mean new territory for everyone to explore, even if it means additional dangers to the first explorers. The diving community has always been slow to respect those who push back the recreational boundaries. Climbers, cavers, yachtsmen and the like operate in environments that are no more terrible, their sports are no more complex, and the dangers no less vital. They are just accepted as part of the risk, part of why people rise to their challenge. The key thing in all these activities is to make sure you understand the risks, that you plan for them, and are properly trained and prepared for them. Only then can you be respected for what you do and, beyond that, it should be up to you.

Diving in itself is not a competitive sport – octopush and the occasional photographic or spearfishing competitions excepted – nor should it be. But it should be allowed to develop, and its boundaries should not be set in concrete by anyone. Unless we continually develop our training procedures, unless we continually accept positive change, then the real benefits of new equipment, new practices, and of a new understanding of physiology and diving science, will *never* reach the recreational diver. This book was written to try and make people think about advanced diving practices, about the inevitabilty of and the neccesity for change. About the need for a reappraisal of who sets the boundaries, or indeed whether they need to be set at all. How we react to the changes will influence how we teach people to dive.

Rob Palmer, Neighbourne, 1994.

"...*there are many issues surrounding a dive which must be taken into consideration before the diver makes the decision to conduct such a dive. These include, but are not limited to, water depth, temperature, visibility, currents, and the diver's physical and mental preparedness, experience, training, and other equipment.*

It is the diver's responsibility to ensure that they have evaluated all the risks and are prepared to accept them. Further, that they have acquired all of the training, and are properly equipped, and have done the necessary planning.

Divers are, in the end, responsible not only for themselves and their actions, but for their families and those whom they love and those who depend on them. They're not only responsible for exploring the underwater world properly, but for getting back safely and passing on the knowledge gained from their experiences."

Dick Long
President, DUI

CHAPTER ONE

What is technical diving?

TECHNICAL DIVING is the use of advanced and specialised equipment and techniques to enable the diver to gain access to depth, dive time, and specific underwater environments more safely than might otherwise be possible.

Safety is, of course, a comparative concept. Most of what we call technical diving might justifiably be regarded as being of higher potential risk than the more normal diving environment of SCUBA enthusiasts, typified by a dive of under an hour at 20 metres, the "no-stop" zone.

Within this book, there are sections which deal with areas that national diving organisations may find difficult to accept since their primary role in life is the safe training of unskilled amateur divers, Many of the practices mentioned here are not recommended by such organisations. But that does not mean that they are unsafe when used by experienced and trained divers. They are advanced techniques, there for those who already have a high degree of diving competence, and have the physical and psychological abilities to proceed further.

This book is not a training manual. It is a book of counsel, a general compendium of experience and technique that has been developed by people who dive beyond the limits of normal recreational diving, and beyond the training normally offered by the major training organisations. This first edition comes out at a time when diving is going through its first real revolution for many years, when the very gases we are breathing are changing, when our understanding of diving physiology is coming out of the closet, and when the quality and complexity of diving equipment is at a level that allows significant advances in human "hands-on" exploration of the underwater world.

THE BASIC RULES OF DIVING

- Breathe in, breathe out, slowly and regularly
- Breathe out when you come up
- Come up slowly
- Carry enough of the proper gas
- Stay warm

Perhaps the most important lesson to be learned is that progress is continuous. Diving is a sport that should have few rules, other than the primary life savers (breathe in, breathe out, slowly and regularly; breathe out when you come up; come up slowly; carry enough of the proper gas; stay warm). It should have a lot of guidelines, based on experience and common sense, and these should be in a continual process of change as techniques, equipment and experience progress. But guidelines can only work if those they are guiding are responsible in their interpretation. Within this world of equipment, experience and technique, the most fallible single component is you, the diver.

Technical diving as a concept began a few years ago in the USA. People have been doing this sort of diving on both sides of the Atlantic for decades, diving in caves, on deep wrecks, under ice, and simply going deep for fun. Breathing mixtures other than air have been in common use in such circles for years. These communities of technical explorers were usually unrecognised by the major training organisations, and their actions, when reported, usually attracted criticism rather than praise. But these people continually fed technical expertise back into the sport diving field, they invented equipment ... the octopus regulator, buoyancy compensators, line reels, crossover manifolds, redundant gas systems ... that made not only their own diving safer, but that also found its way into the sport diving field.

People took up technical diving for a variety of reasons. For some, there was a definite purpose – they were photographers or film makers, who needed to find new subjects or stay down longer; they were wreck divers, who wished to go deeper; they were cave divers, who wished to penetrate further into the flooded underworld; they were sport divers who simply wished to explore more, to develop their own personal boundaries and experience beyond the limits imposed on them by their training organisations. From all these groups and more came the ranks of technical divers, the "professional amateur" whose urge is not driven by a macho desire to impress, but by the simple and utterly justifiable wish to be better, safer and more aware and, above all, to develop their skills and themselves. If you belong in the last camp, or wish to belong, this book is for you. If the macho streak is your driving force, put it down and forget it. You'll get us all into trouble.

Who makes a good technical diver?

Safe divers are divers who take themselves seriously. They accept that no-one can learn everything at once, or learn it just from books. They develop their skills slowly, over years, a bit at a time. They know their own limits, they know when they are coming close to exceeding them, and they know when to back off, and when to return. Their ability to cope with stress is high, they can visualise most problems before they arise, and they can also visualise (and put into practice) the solutions. They understand their equipment and its limitations, and they understand the limitations imposed on them by their own physiology. They have open minds and are always willing to learn. Safe technical diving, one might say, is largely a question of attitude.

So, develop an attitude. Ask yourself some basic questions. Why do you want to develop your diving skills? What are you prepared to sacrifice? How much are you prepared to learn? How long are you prepared to spend learning?

I am not sure that there is any one correct answer but I cannot help feeling that if the answer to any of these questions is something like: "Because I want to go deeper and get more bits of brass", then you are reading this book for the wrong reasons. If it is something like: "Because I want my diving to be safer and my boundaries to be stretched", then you are on the right track.

Technical diving, whether it's using nitrox or other gas mixtures to increase depth or bottom time, or developing safe solo diving or deep diving techniques, is as potentially dangerous as letting an untrained driver loose in a Formula One car. Before you are considered safe to go out on the track there is a great deal to learn, and you should never stop being prepared to learn, and never assume you know it all. You never will. And before stretching your underwater horizons further, you must first learn to cope with yourself.

The psychology of stress

Study carefully an annual report of "fatal diving accidents" and try to find a common denominator. Why did these people have problems? Was it their equipment? Was it the environment? Was it their dive plan, or their level of experience, or the quality of their training? Maybe it was a bit of one or all of these. But you can be sure that in almost every instance, stress played a major role. And in most, it was probably the fatal factor.

Again, ask yourself a few questions. How far can you swim in full deep diving gear? How long can you hold your breath? How far away from your buddy do you normally swim? How often do you practice emergency techniques? Or maintaining breathing rhythms? To what degree does your air consumption increase when you are under extreme stress? Ask yourself how you would have coped.

Stress is the number one killer in diving. We experience it at some point on every dive. It may be on getting in or out of the water, on descent or ascent, or in swimming around on the bottom in the cold and dark. During most dives you are already under a fair degree of stress. If something goes wrong, anxiety levels can rise rapidly, and can spark off any of a number of potentially lethal situations.

Examine the symptoms of extreme stress. A high breathing rate, often accompanied by panting. Extreme nervousness. Dimmed awareness of surroundings, perceptual narrowing, increasing lack of control of your movements. Hands up everyone who's encountered one or more of these during a dive? Did you still feel completely in control of things, able to respond to the situation? Or did you get out of it more by luck than good judgment? If the latter, then hopefully at least you learned something from the experience. For many of us, the only real way to learn is through experience. It's a shame that we too rarely learn by analysing the experiences of others.

A bit of stress on a dive is no bad thing. It keeps your adrenalin level a little higher, and allows you to respond to situations more rapidly. Most psychologists agree that a bit of stress is actually good for you. If you can keep it under control at all times, the quality of your diving will improve beyond measure.

Too much stress is bad. It can actually kill you, all by itself. Panic breathing can abnormally expand your lungs, pressing on and restricting the flow of blood to the heart. This in turn interrupts the flow of oxygenated blood to your brain, and can render you unconscious. Your mouthpiece may fall out, and you may drown. Or, driven by panic, an emergency ascent can produce an embolism.

There are two main types of stress, psychological and physiological – mind and body. They generally interact to some degree, and it is quite possible for one to trigger the other. Psychological stress is not always caused by the environment, though darkness, poor visibility, depth, disorientation and time pressures are key contributors. The source of stress may be your own acts, or an unusually high level of support demanded of you by your diving partners.

Physiological stress is usually an environmental response – high or low temperatures, currents, incorrect weighting, over-exertion, exhaustion, or narcosis. It is usually easier to anticipate these aspects of stress, and to do something about them before you enter the water.

A well-trained diver's ability to cope with stress is usually good. In an inexperienced or poorly-trained diver, the period between slight apprehension and utter panic can be seconds. Stress can be coped with, but by the time stress becomes panic, it is usually too late to do anything about it.

How to cope with stress

The key word in stress management is anticipate. Few things happen to you underwater that cannot be anticipated. Some potential problems are common to all dives, such as running out of air, over staying bottom time, equipment failure, etc. Others are dive specific, like getting lost in a wreck, strong currents, losing a shotline, etc. Spend some of your spare time anticipating what might happen, and how you would solve it. If you run out of air, have you an alternate source (and I don't mean an octopus rig)? How quickly can you reach the other second stage? Is there somewhere you could fasten it that would make access easier? If you get lost in a wreck, do you have a guide line near you to lead you out? Why not? Do you know how to lay one safely? Why not? If you get trapped in a fishing line, can you always reach your knife? Is it worth taking a spare knife? Where would you carry it? What do you do before starting to cut yourself free?

The answer to the last question, and the first thing to do in all high-stress situations, is to stop what you're doing immediately, if possible. Relax. Get your breathing rate down. (If that means getting a spare regulator into your mouth, then do this and then stop and get your breathing under control.) Examine your situation, and your surroundings. Orientate yourself . Only when you are ready, and in control, should you attempt anything else.

That might sound a little too perfect. There are times when immediate action is essential, but unless something is instantly life-threatening, you must always get as much control of yourself as possible before getting yourself into a worse mess. Stop, breathe, think. It is amazing how quickly a degree of perspective can return, and how much comparatively easier it is to solve the problem if you do these three things. It's also amazing how quickly things go progressively more wrong if you don't. This has been called "falling into the incident pit", or, in blunter terms, a "cluster f**k". The chance for cumulative mishap is immense if you give way to panic. Underwater, panic can be fatal.

The trick is to never get into such situations in the first place. Increase the odds in your favour by the use of appropriate equipment, proper dive planning, and by diving within your level of capability on the day. Levels of capability are affected by many things, and can not be regarded as a constant. Just because you did this sort of dive, or maybe the very dive itself, once before, it does not follow that you are capable of doing it now. Your level of fitness or acclimatisation may have changed. You may be tired, stressed at work or at home, and your gear may be unfamiliar. Your buddy may be different, and the weather might be less favourable. No two dives are the same. Be honest in your appraisal of the particular situation, and alter your plans accordingly.

It is also important to watch for signs of stress in your companions. Unless you are diving alone, it is often easier for you to recognise stress in someone else, than it is for them to accept things are getting out of control. The signs of stress are usually straightforward: a lack of reaction to events; shaking; erratic movements; wide, staring eyes; pre-occupation with something trivial; disorientation. If you see such behaviour during a dive, stop, and abort the

REDUCING STRESS

- Dive within your limits
- Choose partners you can trust, with comparable experience
- Improve your diving skills
- Anticipate problems before they arrive, and practice solving them
- Learn all you can about the dive site before the dive
- Do not cut corners in training
- Dive with the proper equipment for the dive, and be familiar with its use
- Take adequate air/gas supplies
- If something goes wrong –
  STOP, BREATHE, THINK, DO

dive. You may even see some signs of stress before the diver enters the water, in which case the dive plan should be abandoned or changed to suit. Remember that levels of competence may be reduced according to how the diver is feeling on the day, and the level of recent experience. If the dive means that much to you, you will make the effort to come back another day. If you cannot come back, it was not worth dying for anyway.

CHAPTER TWO

The physical environment

BEFORE you enter the water, you should understand the physiological needs of technical diving. For the moment, we will exclude the physiological effects of different gas mixtures, which are covered in later sections, and concentrate on the basic environmental parameters you will encounter and have to cope with during a technical dive.

Thermal protection

One of the the basic problems is that of temperature. Unless you are diving in a very unusual locality, the water you are in will be colder than your body temperature. The longer you stay in it, the more significant that difference will become. Even comparatively warm tropical waters can cause hypothermia if your exposure is long enough. Anything below 34C is "cold" as far as body heat loss is concerned, so you need an adequate degree of thermal protection to make temperature a minor problem on a dive. If you become cold, your susceptibility to stress, narcosis, decompression illness and a number of associated problems will increase dramatically. Your ability to carry out manipulative tasks will disappear. You will reach a point at which you cannot physically function any more.

This phenomenon is also known as "unearned fatigue". The lowering of the temperature in muscle and body tissues below the norm over a period of time reduces the body's ability to function normally. A diver suffering from unearned fatigue is limited in the ability to respond to internal or external stimuli, and is susceptible to a wide variety of illnesses. Thermal debt is cumulative, as the body takes a long time to return to its normal thermal balance. It may not have enough time to recuperate fully between dives in multi-day diving operations, and then repeated in-water exposure only makes things worse. You become more susceptible to hypothermia than at the beginning of the dive period.

Equally, you should not become too warm. Hyperthermia (the adverse affect of heat) can cause collapse and physiological stress during a

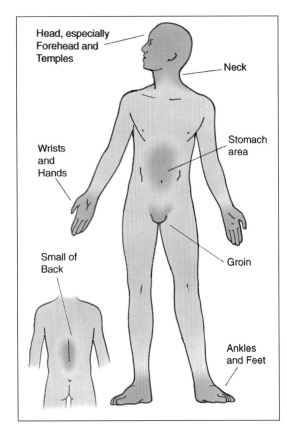

Body heat loss areas.

Head, especially Forehead and Temples

Neck

Wrists and Hands

Stomach area

Groin

Small of Back

Ankles and Feet

dive, and can significantly contribute to decompression illness. Your thermal protection should be adequate to maintain your body temperature at all depths during your dive, not making you hyperthermic before the dive, nor after you leave the water. Decompression illness can be induced virtually instantly by over-exertion or over-heating just after a dive due to the rapid stimulation of blood-flow.

Basically, staying appropriately warm is just as important on technical dives as is carrying enough of the right gas to breathe.

Wetsuits

For the warmest water diving, a lycra "skin" or a thin wetsuit may well be sufficient. The role of the covering here is as much one of environmental protection as a thermal barrier. For most people, little significant thermal loss will be encountered in waters over 21C (70F) when wearing a 5-8mm thick wetsuit. There will be thermal loss, however, in colder waters, or on repetitive dives, or on deep dives, where the thickness of the neoprene is reduced by the compression of the bubbles. Long decompressions, where bodily activity is reduced, can also make you colder. Make sure the thickness of your suit provides adequate insulation at all times.

The key factors to consider with wetsuit use are:
● the temperature of the water
● the depth of the dive
● the duration of the dive
● the construction of the suit

Your own diving experience should indicate how comfortable you feel in a wetsuit at varying water temperatures. Usually, for short deep dives, or reasonably long shallow dives, a wetsuit of appropriate construction may well be sufficient. Appropriate construction means, firstly, that it fits well – a wetsuit is supposed to reduce the flow of water past the skin, and an ill-fitting wetsuit does not do that. Equally, a too-tight wetsuit restricts breathing and circulation, and can thus cause other problems, for example with CO_2 build-up. Water flow should be kept to a minimum by using a minimum number of well-placed zips that do not overlap, a dual thickness of neoprene over core body parts, a good, well-fitting hood that covers the forehead and does not expose the neck, and close-fitting, smooth neoprene seals at wrists and ankles. Bootees and gloves should be worn. The main areas of heat loss in body exposure are the key areas to protect. The body core should have at least 10mm of neoprene covering it for temperate or cold water diving. The construction of the suit should include first glueing the panels together and then sewing using the cup-stitching method, which does not penetrate through the material, thus producing a waterproof seam. Any seam which has

A wetsuit for technical diving.

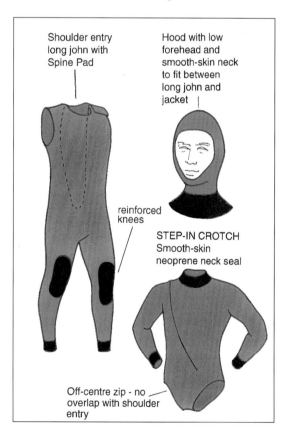

Shoulder entry long john with Spine Pad

Hood with low forehead and smooth-skin neck to fit between long john and jacket

reinforced knees

STEP-IN CROTCH
Smooth-skin neoprene neck seal

Off-centre zip - no overlap with shoulder entry

stitches going from the outside through to the inside is virtually useless as water will flow along the stitch holes into the suit.

Drysuits

For most technical diving operations, a drysuit is essential. It provides, with appropriate insulation, not only a good thermal barrier between you and the environment, but also a degree of buoyancy control.

Simply buying the best you can afford at the time may prove to be no more than a stop-gap measure, and more expensive in the long run. Look at what sort of diving you intend to do, and to what depths you will be venturing. Expanded neoprene suits are fine for shallow cold water dives, but will not be as efficient at depth. The neoprene collapses under pressure, and what may be warm with minimal underwear at 10 metres may be hypothermic at 50 metres after only a few minutes.

Experience has shown that, for advanced diving, materials such as crushed or collapsed neoprene or heavy-duty membranes are most suitable. The construction of the suit is also important: it should be a sufficiently loose fit to make swimming and arm-stretching easy, but not so loose that it requires a lot of inflation gas for buoyancy, or creates excessive drag while swimming. The material should be tear and puncture resistant. A suit which can be donned by the user alone offers some advantage.

Do think of the environment in which you will be using the suit. If you plan to work in overhead environments (such as wrecks, caves, or under ice) then the standard latex wrist and neck seals may not be sufficiently robust. Either replace them with thicker, heavy-duty latex, or with smooth-skin foam neoprene. Wearing long-sleeved gauntlet-style gloves will help to protect wrist seals, and a well-fitting hood, if not already attached to the suit, will help protect the neck seal. If you have reason to be particularly concerned about seal failure, think about replacing the fixed seals with cuff rings and a neck ring, where the seals (latex) are attached to the cuffs and neck by O-ring pressure or a clamp. This allows a torn seal to be easily and rapidly replaced in the field.

For rapid puncture repair, there are proprietary clamp devices like the Rampatch, which can be re-used and which might make the difference between an extremely cold and hazardous dive and a safe, warm one. Maintain a drysuit properly – if you can see that a repair will soon be necessary, repair it before it goes. Underwater failure of a seam, a seal or an ancillary device can have extremely serious consequences.

Drysuits should not be regarded as the sole means of buoyancy control. Whilst you will obviously need to adjust the volume of air inside the suit as depth changes, you should be capable of maintaining buoyancy control by means of a separate device. Which you chose as your primary source is up to you. There is much to be said for having only one dump valve to operate on ascent, and using the separate buoyancy device as a primary source will undoubtedly increase the complexity of the ascent, since you will need, from time to time, to operate both dump valves.

Where on your suit you mount these valves is also worth some consideration. Wherever they are, both inlet and exhaust valves need to be readily

The Rampatch

accessible at all times of the dive. If you are using several regulators on a mixed gas dive, or a jacket-type BC, then your chest may already be cluttered, and finding an inflation valve may be awkward. Though the upper sternum is the standard place to site inflation valves, and may be adequate for your needs, other options include the thigh, at the point at which your hand naturally falls (you may need a longer low-pressure inflation hose for this if you do not have a separate waist or leg-mounted suit-inflation cylinder), or you might place it on your upper right arm.

Exhaust valves are commonly mounted on the left shoulder, where air can be readily vented, or occasionally on the wrist or lower forearm.

It is possible to fit a secondary buoyancy device inside a drysuit, either on the chest or upper back, with separate inflation and exhaust valves. A chest device is perhaps the easiest, where the secondary inflation/ deflation valves can be placed on the upper sternum, allowing the main suit valves to be placed on shoulders or thigh. This secondary bag also provides a certain amount of insulation, but should not be made of expanded neoprene because of the extra buoyancy incurred. It is difficult to provide enough redundant buoyancy in such a system to make it equal in lift to the primary system.

Additional options for technical diving include sealed dry-gloves and hoods; comfort zips (or even catheter attachments for extremely long dives); pockets for decompression tables, slates, knives and/or tools; knee and elbow pads for contact diving (eg cave, wreck or high-current), and possibly a pouch for a 2-litre suit-inflation cylinder.

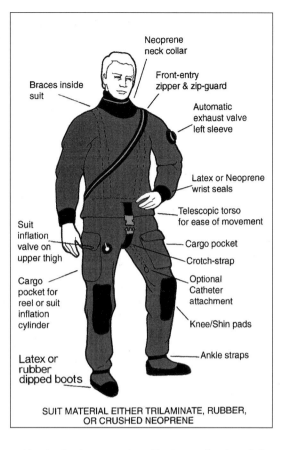

Neoprene neck collar

Front-entry zipper & zip-guard

Braces inside suit

Automatic exhaust valve left sleeve

Latex or Neoprene wrist seals

Telescopic torso for ease of movement

Suit inflation valve on upper thigh

Cargo pocket

Crotch-strap

Optional Catheter attachment

Cargo pocket for reel or suit inflation cylinder

Knee/Shin pads

Ankle straps

Latex or rubber dipped boots

SUIT MATERIAL EITHER TRILAMINATE, RUBBER, OR CRUSHED NEOPRENE

Features of a drysuit for technical diving.

Underwear

Any drysuit is only as efficient as the garments worn beneath it. Few drysuits other than expanded neoprene suits provide much if anything in the way of integral thermal insulation. Membrane suits can actually draw heat away from the body by thermal conduction.

Thermal insulation is usually measured in Clo. A Clo unit is the amount of insulation needed to keep an "average" human being in thermal balance in air when the temperature is 20C, the relative humidity is less than 50%, and the air movement no more than 6 metres/minute. This is often regarded as the equivalent of a three-piece business suit.

To put this in an underwater perspective, a 5mm closed-cell neoprene wetsuit has a surface Clo value of 1.8, which is dramatically reduced to 0.25 at a depth of 30 metres. Point made?

Where undergarments are concerned, experience has shown that a layer system is most efficient. The base layer is usually a silk or lightweight wicking material such as Damart® or polypropylene-weave liners. This is not windproof or waterproof, but should wick condensation and sweat away from the body, thus avoiding cold or wet spots.

On top of this base layer is a further layer of more insulative material, either fibre-pile or Thinsulate®, or something with similar performance characteristics based on slight loft, that will trap air and thus provide some warmth. Another option is an open-cell foam, such as that used in Viking® underwear. This is effectively a polyurethane sponge, resistant to compression because of its open-cell structure. It is buoyant when dry, and has a Clo rating of 1.2. It does not stretch, and thus has to be cut loosely to allow normal movement. In most cases, open-cell foam underwear is perfectly adequate, but it is unfortunately all but useless when wet. If the suit leaks badly, the foam rapidly becomes saturated, loses its buoyancy, and will actually conduct heat away from the body through thermal conductivity. It is not a serious option for long dives, where extended decompressions might have to take place in a punctured or leaking suit.

Similarly, fibre-pile garments (also known as "woolly bears") which may be more than adequately warm when dry, have greatly reduced thermal values when wet. Most pile diving undergarments are made of polyester, which feels good, and is compression resistant at depth. An undersuit of 16oz polyester fibre-pile has a Clo of 1.65 when dry, and as long as it stays dry, is perfectly warm. Polyester does not form lint balls (pilling) like nylon fibre-pile, which have been known to jam exhaust valves on drysuits. Do be aware which you are buying. Unfortunately, expense may not be a guide to performance, and it is not simply a question of how good they feel and look on the surface when dry.

For most technical diving purposes, Thinsulate® has become regarded as the material against which other fabrics are measured. Whilst a little stiffer and heavier than some fabrics, Thinsulate® is manufactured from polyolefin microfibres, in various weaves for various purposes. The only type suitable for diving is "Type B". What makes Thinsulate® different is that it is hydrophobic – it repels water.

B-grade Thinsulate® comes in two thicknesses, B-200 which is 0.5cm thick, with a Clo of 0.9, and B-400, which is 1cm thick and has a Clo value of 1.8. The microfibres, even when wet, absorb only 1% by weight of water, and thus even in the case of a drysuit flooding completely, will still supply a considerable degree of insulation, more so than any other.

Thinsulate® is usually used in conjunction with other materials in undergarments, and usually has a nylon or Pertex® (a microfibre wicking material) outer for wind-proofing, and to make it easier to slip the drysuit on over the top, and an inner layer of fleece or fibre-pile. Different suits are designed for different temperature and diving conditions, so make sure that the manufacturer states what conditions the garment is designed for, and that these meet your needs. For technical diving purposes involving long or deep exposures, B-400 Thinsulate® should be regarded as the standard basic material for your undersuit.

Suit inflation systems

The common way for SCUBA divers to inflate drysuits is usually by connecting a low pressure hose directly to the first stage of the regulator, and inflating from the main air supply. On deep or long dives, the amount of gas used can seriously eat into your gas reserves, so some other method should be used. The simplest thing is to carry a separate pony bottle containing a sufficient supply of gas (2-3 litres) to ensure that the suit's buoyancy can be regularly adjusted throughout the dive, whilst retaining enough gas to allow an emergency ascent to take place. It is bad practice to run suit and BC

inflation from the same cylinder. If the first stage fails, or you run out of gas in that cylinder, your eggs are all in the same basket, and you are going to have difficulty getting to the surface.

Some technical divers – especially those diving very deep or in cold waters – have been experimenting with argon as a suit inflation gas. Its benefits are its relatively low cost (it is used as an inert atmosphere for welding, and is readily available) and, due to its greater molecular density, a better degree of thermal efficiency. There is some question as to whether it may be absorbed through the skin on long dives, creating potential decompression problems, but experience has not yet shown this to be a problem.

If you use Argon, the cylinder should be painted in the appropriate colour (turquoise in the UK) and the cylinder valve should have a connection other than a standard regulator connection. At no point should it be possible to connect a SCUBA regulator to a cylinder containing an unbreathable gas.

Divers using trimix or heliox mixtures should NEVER run suit inflation from their breathing tank – the lower molecular density of helium increases its conductivity, and body heat will be lost more quickly.

AVOID INFLATING A SUIT FROM A BREATHING CYLINDER CONTAINING ANY AMOUNT OF HELIUM IN THE GAS MIXTURE

CHAPTER THREE

Equipment

ONE OF THE BASIC assumptions of technical diving is that you are placing yourself beyond the limits normally imposed by sport diving organisations. This may mean that you will have to re-think your attitude to your choice and configuration of diving equipment. The effect of various gas mixtures on equipment is dealt with in a later section, but here we'll take a look at the techniques that have evolved to make deep or high exposure diving safer and more practical.

In most high exposure diving environments, you are placing yourself beyond reach of the surface, by either depth or time (ie, decompression) constraints, by entering an overhead environment (eg, wreck, cave, ice), or by any combination of the above. This means you are extremely unlikely to be able to breath-hold back to the surface, and therefore it cannot be regarded as a "safe haven". If you encounter life-threatening problems, you have to sort them out yourself in order to survive.

Solo diving

Though solo diving is frowned upon in sport diving circles, the solo ethic is the one that may save your life. In reality, every dive is a solo dive. For much of it, your are probably out of touch with your buddy, if you have one,

Solo diving techniques have been developed by cave divers.

either because you are looking in different directions or you are too far apart to reach him or her in an emergency. By the time some major crisis has occurred and you have reached each other, the state of panic may well have superseded rationality for one or the other of you and you simply have the reassurance of dying in company.

You should NEVER have to rely on any companion to save your life. They can on occasion assist you out of embarrassing situations, or help you recover from a crisis, but they should not be essential to your survival. It's not fair to them. You should always be able to get out of any underwater situation you may find yourself in. At worst, if you anticipate that a particular problem may arise, you should, by dint of being aware of it, be briefed and practised in the necessary response.

Cave divers have practiced the technique of solo diving for years. They habitually use at least two separate breathing systems – two tanks, two regulators, two contents gauges. Neither system is ever breathed dry during a dive; there is always enough gas to get you back to base in either set, even if it means returning with a full third of your supply (see 'Rule of Thirds' later). It should be obvious to all divers that running out of air underwater is cardinal stupidity, not an accident. This system of multiple redundancy is taken further where necessary. The diver carries two of any item where the failure of loss of one might prove fatal. Two decompression computers (same make and model), or two dive timers, two knives, two torches (maybe more in an overhead environment) and, if the situation warrants, even two masks. "Hard" decompression tables (always using the same set of tables as the computer) are used to back up the machine. Two buoyancy devices – either a drysuit and buoyancy compensator, or a wetsuit and twin "wings" – give an additional source of buoyancy control on deep dives, where a means of controlling ascent and descent is vital.

The emphasis is on self-reliance, and on a complete understanding of the equipment selected and being used.

Regulators

Regulators, or 'demand valves', are much-abused pieces of equipment which take the blame for many of the self-inflicted wounds of diving. Recent publicity in the diving press has shown that many of the regulators on the market today are not suitable for extreme breathing rates, or breathing at depth, and that some have difficulty providing an adequate air flow under stress conditions at the surface. Clearly, not all regulators are suitable for technical diving.

In recent years, performance standards have been introduced by various organisations, firstly the US Navy and more recently the European Standards Organisation (CEN).The breathing rate charts published from time to time in the diving press show the breathing characteristics of most of the popular regulators on the market in terms of these performance standards. Check the latest edition of these rating lists before you buy a regulator, or ask your dealer or the manufacturer for the performance data.

The inference is obvious: avoid the poor performers, and go for the best. Do not make false economies or support brand names out of misplaced loyalty. Do, however, take a few other things into account. Such as, can the regulator be uprated easily for nitrox/oxygen use; how many high and low pressure ports does it have; is it environmentally sealed for use in cold or dirty environments? Can you carry out basic maintainance yourself, or does it require special tools and a bench testing system to change an O-ring?

Take care with hose layouts.

You should be able to maintain your own equipment in reasonable order. It helps you to know your equipment better, and understand the reasons for any potential limitations.

Remember, though, that if you tinker with your own equipment without having the necessary training then you will invalidate the manufacturer's guarantee. If a more comprehensive service is needed, take your regulator to a service centre you trust, where the service personnel have attended the full manufacturer's service course in the maintenance of your regulator, and try to avoid their busy periods. If you wish to carry out the regular servicing your regulator requires, then attend the manufacturer's course yourself to ensure that you achieve the necessary competence. You will need a few extra tools and a medium pressure gauge, but it could be worth the investment. It is essential that the periodic servicing is carried out only by those who are trained and competent in these techniques.

For technical diving, a regulator needs to have good breathing performance across the board. DIN (screw-fitting) first stages are better suited to technical diving than the more traditional A-clamp; they are less likely to become unseated when knocked, and can cope better with new high-pressure cylinders. If you are using 300bar cylinders make sure you buy high-pressure DIN first-stages, suitable for 300 bar cylinders. 200 bar DIN first-stages do not fit the high-pressure 300 bar cylinder valves, though 300 bar first stages do fit the lower pressure (200bar) cylinder valves.

Take time to set up your low- and high-pressure hoses in a manner that avoids a mess behind your back that offers the potential for ensnarement, or damage to hoses. Kinks in hoses, too-long hoses, or over-stretched hoses, cause unnecessary wear and tear and may become prone to failure and/or entanglement. Use angled adaptors in high or medium pressure ports if necessary.

When using double cylinders (which, for technical divers, is much of the time), configure one regulator for one cylinder and one for the other. Try and get opposing regulators, one which is set to come at you from the left, and one from the right. This is most easily done by using at least one regulator like those in the Poseidon range, the Oceanic Omega, or Apeks ST5000, all of which when set up properly are suitable for technical diving. Most other regulators approach from the right, though some can be adapted to come from the left, or have octopus second stages which can replace the standard second stage (eg. Scubapro Air II, Apeks Octo +, SeaQuest Air Source, etc.) THOUGH IT SHOULD BE REMEMBERED THAT THESE OCTOPUS SECOND STAGES MAY NOT BE "Class A" REGULATORS.

Regulator setup comparison.

MAKE SURE YOU CAN ALWAYS REACH YOUR CYLINDER VALVES TO TURN THEM ON OR OFF IN AN EMERGENCY

Cylinder configuration

For deep decompression diving, or overhead environment diving, it is essential to have at least two independently-valved cylinders. To be blunt, a 15 litre cylinder and a 3 litre pony (a combination used by many divers) do not provide enough spare air to meet most eventualities. Two 9 or 10 litre cylinders would be a much safer configuration, each with its own regulator, to avoid the problems of regulator failure on a main cylinder. Crossover manifolds (DIN) are one way of avoiding the need for changing mouthpieces underwater, though the latter honestly presents no real problem and allows you to make sure all your equipment is working throughout the dive. It also ensures that you monitor your air consumption and reserves; it is bad practice to breathe one cylinder almost dry before changing over. The technical diving norm is to follow the cave diving practice of breathing each cylinder down by one third at a time, balancing the reserve in each cylinder, and surfacing with enough air in each to meet any crisis for you or a buddy during the final stages of the dive – especially if decompression is planned.

There are several types of crossover manifold if you feel you prefer to use one. A-clamps are less well adapted to technical diving , are less safe than DIN valves when used in overhead environments, and are not suitable for high-pressure cylinders (above 232 bar). Some manifolds have only one regulator take off; these are unsafe and offer no redundancy in the case of regulator failure. The best have separate cylinder valves, allowing each cylinder or each regulator to be isolated from the system if necessary, and an additional isolator valve in the centre, allowing the cylinders themselves to be isolated in the event of a tank or valve O-ring failure. Thus, in the event of a regulator failure, the other regulator can still have access to all the remaining air. There is much to be said for this system, though, in certain cases, failure of the isolation valve and then failure of the associated first stage has meant that divers have lost most or all of their air to the surrounding water. In fairness, however, such accidents are very unusual, and most of these accidents would not have happened if DIN first stages had been chosen to begin with.

For long deep dives, or long overhead environment dives, multiple cylinder configurations are commonly used. Triples or quads are worn on the back, and one or more cylinders may be chest or side mounted. Frequently such additional cylinders may contain "travel mix" or oxygen for decompression (see Section 4) and some way of distinguishing these cylinders and regulators is necessary. Colour coding of cylinders and regulators according to the gas mixture is the commonly accepted technique. Oxygen cylinders and regulators are green in the USA, black with a white neck in the UK, and nitrox cylinders are yellow with a green band at the neck. Heliox or trimix cylinders should also be clearly distinguished, and appropriate stickers are available from TDI, IANTD and ANDI (see reference section for addresses).

It is very important on mixed gas dives that all cylinders should unambiguously indicate their contents, including the percentages of oxygen and helium where relevant. Certain mixtures are unsafe at some depths, and misuse will, at the very least, compromise decompression schedules.

Backpacks for triples or quads can easily be made, either by pre-forming stainless steel bands or by adapting a double back pack cam-band sys-

Convertible DIN and A-clamp manifolds.

AN INTRODUCTION TO TECHNICAL DIVING

Opposite: Stainless steel cylinder bands and back pack cam system.

tem. To ensure that you know which regulator goes with which, use matching colours, or coloured electrical tape, to match first stages with contents gauges. Try to breathe equally from each appropriate cylinder in turn, otherwise you may find strange things happening to your buoyancy or trim if you start at one side and breathe all down to empty!

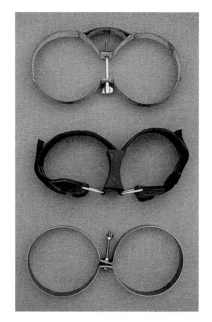

Regulator coding

When you are in the water the most significant part of the coding scheme is the matching of regulators and contents gauges to gas mixtures and/or cylinders. Even when using a single gas mix, if separate cylinders are used you must be able to say which regulator matches which cylinder. Colour coding is a commonly accepted practice, with regulators matching as closely as possible the cylinder or gas colours. Regulators can be matched to contents gauges either by purchasing appropriately coloured consoles and regulator trimmings, or by using coloured electrical tape. Where decompression or travel gas mixtures contain levels of oxygen which may be hazardous to breathe at particular depths, some form of immediate identification is necessary. Such regulators should not only be clearly distinguished visually, perhaps by adding a written label to state the mixture, but should be placed so that it is impossible to breathe from them by accident. This could be by placing them in a pocket, clipping them in an accessible but out-of-the-way place (such as on or near the hip), or by ensuring that they contain a visual plug in the mouthpiece which has to be removed before use, and leaving the cylinder turned off until the decompression has started.

Buoyancy compensators

Colour-coded regulators.

With all this pile of equipment, you will need extra buoyancy. Depending on what type of cylinders you have available, your buoyancy may change by several kilos during the course of the dive. During the early part of the dive you will need additional buoyancy to counteract the weight of the gas carried, whilst you will need to carry sufficient weight to counteract the positive buoyancy of the system when the gas is used. It takes some practice to get this right, and it is essential to accustom yourself to the system in a pool or in shallow water before using it in earnest. It is possible to distribute weight more evenly by attaching lead to the cylinders, or to shoulder straps. Some divers are even returning to the concept of a chest weight (cast, for example, in an old frying pan!). These should be worn so as not to interfere with breathing or with drysuit valves.

The volume of the buoyancy compensator being used is also crucial; in the worst case it will need to be sufficient to take you and the complete system to the surface during the early part of the dive. Some of the more fashionable BC's are not aimed at this type of diving and may not have enough capacity to do this. You will probably need a minimum of 20-25kg of primary lift in each BC for a deep dive.

Of the buoyancy compensators in use by technical divers, the clear favourite appears to be the "wings" style of BC. This takes the buoyancy behind your back, between you and the cylinders, making for an extremely streamlined rig that sits very comfortably and has the minimum of strapping and obstruction on the chest, another bonus when using multiple regulators and/or chest-mounted stage cylinders. Whilst it is not designed to act as a lifejacket, when used with a drysuit it allows not only unobstructed access to inflation valves, but does keep the diver head up and high above the water at the surface. Under the water, buoyancy is distributed more evenly, allowing a prone swimming position more readily than is possible with some buoyancy compensators.

It is also one of the only devices that allows two compensators to be fitted back to back, even when twinned with a vest-style BC. This is essential when diving deep when a drysuit is not being used

The use of a dedicated cylinder for suit and/or BC inflation has already been mentioned. Direct feed inflation is the norm on technical dives, and few technical divers carry the small "emergency" inflation cylinder common with European BC's, or the CO_2 cartridge more popular in the States. With a properly thought-out "redundant" system, you should have a better and more adequate supply of "emergency" inflation gas than these could ever give in a crisis.

Top: "Wings" style buoyancy compensator; and dedicated direct feed cylinder (below).

Stage cylinders

It is becoming increasingly common, especially on overhead environment or mixed gas dives, to carry one or more stage cylinders. These are usually worn on the chest, and contain additional gas for long shallow dives or for decompression, or a "travel mix" (usually nitrox or air) for the shallower portions of long, deep dives. Gas mixtures and their appropriate use are covered in later sections, but a brief word on how to use stage cylinders is more appropriate here.

The easiest way to carry stage cylinders is to use two stainless steel jubilee clips, each with a non-corrodible karabiner or brass snaplink and clip the cylinder to appropriate points near your waist and shoulder, either on a BC or on an appropriate harness. Low and high pressure hoses on the regulator can be slipped behind elasticated loops on the cylinder (inner tube is fine) to avoid them hanging free and snagging on obstacles. If it is planned to remove the cylinder during the dive and replace it on the return to base, the

cylinder can be slipped between elasticated loops on waist and chest if required.

Take care to set up the stage cylinder so that it offers the minimum possibility for line entanglement. Keep it as streamlined as possible, loop gauges and second stages behind rubber bands, or use short high-pressure hoses, and cover the ends of the jubilee clips with heavy duty insulating or duct tape, or slip them through lightweight hollow climbing tape before tightening down.

If you are undertaking a long deep dive, or any dive requiring decompression, it is good practice to take your decompression gas with you in a separate cylinder, which must not be used during the dive. Do not rely on a stage cylinder hung below the boat – both it and the boat may have disappeared on your return, or you may drift away and lose your contact with it. Surfacing lost, having missed your decompression as well, is simply stupid. Applied Darwinism, some might say.

If your decompression cylinder contains gas with a higher percentage of oxygen than air, mark it and the regulator clearly. Using it at depth by mistake, and thus unwittingly exceeding the oxygen toxicity limits of the mix, could prove fatal.

The illustration below (right) shows a possible set-up for stage decompression diving, where all the cylinders for the dive are carried by the diver. This rig was developed by Richard Pyle, a marine icthyologist who specialised in collecting specimens from betwen 60 and 90 metres, in the region he calls the marine "twilight zone" due to the lack or research so far undertaken within it.

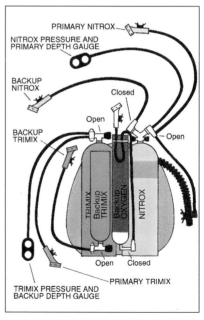

PRIMARY NITROX

NITROX PRESSURE AND
PRIMARY DEPTH GAUGE

BACKUP
NITROX

Closed

Open

BACKUP
TRIMIX

Open

TRIMIX
Backup
TRIMIX
Backup
OXYGEN
NITROX

Open   Closed

PRIMARY TRIMIX

TRIMIX PRESSURE AND
BACKUP DEPTH GAUGE

Above right: Stage cylinder with snap-links. Left: Set-up for stage decompression diving. Right: Richard Pyle's deep cylinder set.

Alternate air sources

A lot of fuzziness exists around what is really meant by an alternate air source. For technical diving, an alternate air source should provide an adequate and continuous, stress-free supply of breathing gas that endangers neither the donor nor the recipient, each of whom should be breathing from separate cylinders. Octopus rigs don't count; they are a useful way of sharing from a single tank at shallow depths, and that is all; they still depend on a single air source and a single first stage, and that is not a fully redundant system. Some first stages are incapable of supplying an adequate flow of gas to two stressed divers. Others, in cold water, may freeze open and free-flow. Some cylinder valves do not even allow enough air to flow into a perfectly adequate first-stage for an octopus rig. Do you know what both your first stage and cylinder valve flow-rates are?

Multiple outlet valve.

High performance inflator/second stages, like Scubapro's Air II, the SeaQuest Air Source or the Apeks Octo+, are really octopus sets, though they do provide an additional back-up at shallow depths. It's dangerous to regard them as a deep primary back-up, even when their performance characteristics show a high depth rating, unless they are attached separately and directly to the second gas source. Even on shallow dives, the use of a double tank valve,allows two regulators to be mounted on the same cylinder. Better to use two first stages and mount your Air II or Octo+ as the second stage on the second valve. And remember, in times of real stress a 3 litre cylinder will be inadequate as a secondary air source, providing only enough air to simply delay real emergency air sharing. A true separate air source should have the same volume as its partner, and should be large enough to cover any emergency. You would not dive to 50 metres on a 3 litre cylinder, so why depend on one that size in an emergency when you are already down there?

It has become the norm in the US, though not yet in the UK and Europe, for the second regulator to be fitted to a 1.5 to 2 metre medium pressure hose.

Two metre hose retained by inner tube.

This allows a second diver to share breathing gas in an emergency without interfering unduly with the donor, the two being able to swim comfortably side by side, or one behind the other, even in a wreck or a cave. Doing this removes another source of stress, and increases the safety of gas sharing immensely. The extra hose length can be easily retained by a piece of inner tube or rubber lab tube on the cylinder, and pulled free if required. The 2 metre hose was originally developed for cave diving, so that an out-of-air diver could swim behind his rescuer in a cave, and pass through restrictions, while both divers remained in contact with the guideline.

Contents gauges and consoles should never, ever be allowed to hang free. Not only do they snag on obstacles or drag along the bottom (spoiling the environment, the equipment and your visibility), but they are not readily visible when you need to see them. High-pressure hoses, snagging at the contents gauge end, can break and the loss of air can get you very quickly into a low air crisis! Clip them to you in a place where they will neither drag nor snag, and where you can see them. Dangling equipment is a sure sign of a thoughtless diver! Remember to colour-code gauges to regulators, wherever confusion may occur, and check them regularly. Let it become second nature.

Ancillary equipment

Ancillary equipment is largely determined by the requirements of the environment and the preferences of the diver involved. Most divers have their favourite make and type of fins, and the only time when style becomes relevant is when fine sediments are involved. Big fins, while they have their place in open water, can kick up more silt if used incorrectly in more confined locations. Masks should be low in both volume and profile and should fit very well – on deep dives you can use up a lot of gas just by mask clearing. It's worth getting one that covers a lot of your forehead as well as being of low volume (hood manufacturers often seem not to realise that the forehead is one of the main points of heat loss) and a good low-volume mask can provide a significant amount of insulation while still offering an excellent field of vision.

Two knives are a must, and should be picked more for their cutting ability than their ability to impress non-divers. Unless they are non-magnetic, keep them away from your compass. If that sounds silly, try holding your knife next to your compass and watch the needle turn. Mount one on the upper arm (left side if you're right-handed) and one on your leg, and secure both to their sheaths by thin bungee-cord. It's easy to drop a knife when highly-stressed. Some divers secure them to the inflator hose on the BC, allowing a degree of access by both hands.

The key thing about all your equipment is to understand it fully, to know its strengths and its weaknesses, and to be able to trust it. Make sure it can cope with the dive, and that, like you, it's in a condition to do so. Then you've only yourself to blame when things go wrong, which is, at least, an improvement.

Rebreathers

Recent developments in rebreather technology mean that in the coming years more and more divers will be using rebreathers not only for technical diving but also recreational diving at all levels.

Rebreathing as a concept has been around for a long time. In the middle ages, various self-contained systems were experimented with, based on bladders full of air or enclosed one-man mobile diving chambers. However, it was not until the early 20th century that rebreather technology began to make an impact. In 1913, German and British companies were experimenting with simple self-contained oxygen and nitrox rebreathers, with some success, and by World War Two oxygen rebreathers were in common military use on both sides. Hans Hass, the underwater pioneer, used one extensively in the Mediterranean in 1942. Shortly afterwards, Cousteau and Gagnan developed the forerunner of modern open-circuit SCUBA. Rebreathers have, therefore, been around much longer than recreational SCUBA diving.

So why haven't rebreathers replaced the air cylinder before now? Surely a system which recycles the diver's gas, leaves few bubbles and makes no noise, which allows use of an automatically oxygen-enriched breathing gas, and which lasts several times as long as conventional SCUBA gear, should walk away with the prizes?

The problem has essentially been one of control. The early rebreathers were manually operated, usually running on pure oxygen, which limited their effective depth to 10 metres or so. The manual system, opening a valve to add more gas when it was demanded, required a fairly high level of training. In addition, the carbon dioxide absorbent used in the early models was an inferior grade of soda lime, which, when wet, had a tendency to

CCR 155 rebreather.

send a caustic solution back up the breathing tube into the diver's lungs. They were not ideal for sports use.

Rebreather development continued into the late 20th century with a move first to nitrox units, then to mixed gas units, such as the Electrolung, the Rexnord CCR-1000, and the Normalair-Garret Deep Dive 500. Sensor technology was improved to the point at which on-line sensors would continuously measure the oxygen content of the gas mix, triggering electronic circuitry which would automatically add oxygen when required. Diluent (air, nitrogen, trimix or helium) was added by a pressure-sensitive valve during descent, and manually if required thereafter. The diver's display unit told him/her when the mixture was at the required oxygen setpoint, and when to take emergency action if it deviated too much. If the system malfunctioned, a secondary display showed each separate sensor reading, and the diver could inject either oxygen or diluent as required to run the unit manually.

The problem by this point was that the military had essentially hijacked the concept, and that rebreathers built to military specifications were expensive. Though these are now filtering back into the commercial market due to increasing demand, the one based on the US Navy version, the CCR155, built by Biomarine Ltd, carries a $10,000 price tag. A few commercial firms toyed with rebreathers as bail-outs for deep saturation dives, but so much had already been invested in umbilical support and bell systems that such expensive new technology was usually considered to be unnecessary.

As computer control systems became more common, and their size shrank, powerful software could be set in small, portable packages to run rebreathers

Early rebreather set.

more efficiently. Sensor technology improved even further, and costs fell. Hardware became more reliable, and good decompression tables were developed for fixed partial pressure use. By the late 1980s several research companies were developing affordable rebreather systems for the commercial and recreational markets.

In 1997, the leading companies are Dräger of Germany, Biomarine, Undersea Technology, Cochran, and Cis-Lunar Development Laboratories in the USA. All are producing affordable systems that will eventually revolutionise sport diving.

Dräger, who produced one of the first oxygen rebreathers in 1913, have developed a number of units for military, commercial and recreational markets. Their recreational model, the Atlantis, has an approximate 140-minute duration and comes in a nitrox version suitable for use throughout the air range to 40 metres. Dräger have a long and continuing involvement with rebreather technology, from the pre-World War One experiments to their later military models. Their Lar V military unit, like the Carleton Technologies O_2 rebreather, the CCR25, provides about three hours of breathing at depths of up to 8 metres, at which point the acceptable O_2 toxicity threshold has been reached, even by military standards.

Semi-closed circuit rebreathers, like Dräger's Atlantis or FGT I/D military models, or Spirotechnique's DC-55, provide a further step to long-duration self-sufficiency. Unlike the more modern closed-circuit systems, they have to have their operating mixtures pre-set, and are thus depth-limited on a dive to dive basis. A semi-closed rebreather works on a constant feed principle, where a slow trickle of pre-mixed gas is constantly fed into the breathing bag, from which it is inhaled, passing through the CO_2 absorbent after exhalation. When pressure builds up in the breathing bag, the excess gas is vented through an exhaust valve into the surrounding water. Because each breath is breathed several times and the flow into the bag is slow, small 3-5 litre cylinders of pre-mix can be made to last several hours.

The major advantage of a closed-circuit rebreather is the use of a constant partial pressure of oxygen, which means that the actual percentage of oxygen in the mixture is varying constantly with depth throughout the dive. This differs from open circuit scuba, where the percentage remains constant but the partial pressure changes. In a rebreather, if the partial pressure of oxygen is set at, say 1.4 bar, then that is what it remains at whatever the depth. At greater depths, oxygen toxicity is kept at bay, and at shallower depths, the mixture breathed is constantly an oxygen-rich one. The duration of the set avoids too long an exposure to the higher partial pressure of oxygen (see Chapter 5), and decompression obligations can be greatly reduced. At 20 metres, for example, over 2 hours can be spent without any decompression requirement at a setpoint of 1.4 bar. Depths of 70-80 metres can be reached without the problems of narcosis on a mixed gas set, though there is by then a reasonably long decompression requirement, and care must be taken not to exceed the duration of the set, especially if the diver wishes to take advantage of the automatic oxygen-rich decompression.

Thermal considerations are also important during long-duration diving of this kind.

The Undersea Technology UT 240, Cochran Prism II and Cis-Lunar Mk 5 systems are controlled by on-board computers, which monitor and continually adjust the gas mixtures throughout the dive. Both have the facility for the diver to select a more oxygen-rich mixture for decompression, if that is appropriate to the dive plan and O_2 exposure times. Display units show the usual readouts – depth, maximum depth, time and elapsed time, O_2 and diluent cylinder contents, and ambient temperature. They also indicate the performance and reading of the oxygen sensors, and track the unit build-up of oxygen exposure to allow pulmonary oxygen toxicity to be avoided.

The computer-control concept undoubtedly works, and the prototypes have been field tested on a number of scientific and cave diving projects.

The pay-off, however, is a need for new techniques to be developed and understood. Buoyancy control at shallow depths is different, and buoyancy gas must be provided by a separate cylinder (which, if large enough, can also be used to provide a redundant bail-out in case the rebreather malfunctions to the point at which on-board redundancy is affected). More needs to be understood by the diver about gas laws, constant partial pressure systems and decompression. Thermal exposure, and new aspects of dive planning (eg, what do you do when you can't follow someone's bubbles from a boat?) need to be learned, as do new aspects of equipment care and maintenance.

Again, none of this is especially difficult, but book learning is no substitute for experience, and proper training procedures should be followed before

Above left: Dräger Atlantis semi-closed circuit rebreather. Above right: Cis-Lunar rebreather.

The Buddy Inspiration closed-circuit rebreather.

using rebreather technology in advanced or recreational diving. No piece of equipment can magically remove the obligation for decompression, environmental protection or dive planning. It can change the requirements, but you still have to learn the new rules.

CHAPTER FOUR

Deep diving

FOR TECHNICAL DIVING purposes, deep diving can be defined as anything over 40 metres. Whilst that is the limit most sport diving organisations place on recreational diving, we must accept that many advanced divers wish to – and do – dive beyond that depth on a regular basis. Unfortunately, few training organisations are prepared to teach safe deep diving techniques, and people die as a result of being untrained in the problems associated with deep diving.

Despite that, it is possible to dive deep in comparative safety, with good health, proper training, a sensible attitude to decompression problems, and a proper use of appropriate gas mixtures.

The main problems that will be encountered in deep diving can be listed simply, in no particular order of priority:

- Nitrogen Narcosis.
- Oxygen toxicity.
- CO_2 blackout.
- Decompression.
- Gas consumption.
- Buoyancy.
- Temperature

To these can be added some of the longer term physiological effects of deep diving (for the sake of completeness), such as aseptic bone necrosis, capillary die-off, and general body stress.

Before we look at how to plan a deep dive safely, it's worth knowing what we're letting ourselves in for.

Nitrogen Narcosis

All divers know what nitrogen narcosis is. As you venture deeper underwater, the narcotic effect of nitrogen at elevated partial pressures makes itself felt insidiously on the mind and body. As far as basic hazards go, gas toxicity, be it nitrogen, carbon dioxide or oxygen based, is perhaps the most important physiological hazard facing the deep diver. Anything that can be done to reduce the effects of gas toxicity is a bonus.

Inert gas narcosis is a result of dissolved nitrogen in the tissues acting as a depressant on the central nervous system. This seems to be proportional to the amount going into solution at a particular partial pressure, and basically nitrogen is not a desirable gas to be breathing at increased partial pressures. The relative narcotic potential of a gas, when expressed in numeric terms, is an indication of this, with the least narcotic gas having the highest number.

Argon, for example, is extremely narcotic with a value of 0.43, nitrogen is rated at 1.0, while helium is one of the least narcotic with a value of 4.26.

Symptoms of nitrogen narcosis are dizziness, personality changes, mood swings, general euphoria and apparent "drunkenness" – or sometimes the opposite – fear and anxiety, loss of co-ordination, numbness of the lips, tunnel vision and, in severe cases, loss of consciousness.

Though the only solution to narcosis is to ascend to a shallower depth, the effects of nitrogen narcosis can be reduced in several ways. At depths down to 40 metres, oxygen-enriched air (Nitrox) can be used to reduce the amount (and hence the partial pressure) of nitrogen in the breathing mix. This is covered in greater detail later, but the payoffs below 40 metres for nitrox are slim. Air is a suitable nitrox mix for depths down to 50 or 60 metres, but beyond that the effects of narcosis are extreme, and oxygen toxicity becomes a problem. Helium can be used as an additional dilutant, making a trimix, to reduce the effect of the nitrogen while still maintaining a healthy partial pressure of oxygen in the mixture. This is an expensive option for open-circuit SCUBA, however, and trimix decompression tables are not yet readily available.

The use of trimix can extend deep diving on open-circuit SCUBA, in relative safety, down to the 80-100 metre level, and extreme SCUBA dives have been made to over 250 metres using such mixtures. The use of trimix requires a far higher degree of dive planning and co-ordination, and a far greater degree of understanding of gas physics, human physiology and specialised decompression schedules than is currently appropriate for recreational diving. Those wishing to dive on trimix require specialised training and equipment that takes them deep into technical diving territory, and they should consider whether the use of open-circuit trimix is worth the cost and commitment involved.

For most air diving purposes, acclimatisation to depth is almost as significant as understanding the full effects of nitrogen itself. Again, there is little substitute for experience, and the best way to deal with narcosis on deep air dives is to do them regularly, and to know your limits. A break of as little as one week can lose most of the acclimatisation, so caution should be taken

A deep wreck dive.

where such a lay-off has taken place. If a regular series of deep dives is envisaged, a gradual build-up over several days is best. Do not assume that because you were well acclimatised the week before, you will still be able to cope with depth several days later.

Tolerance to narcosis varies, even in a single individual, from day to day, especially when the above factors are taken into account. No two dives are alike, and it is a mistake to assume that feeling good at 60 metres one day can mean that you will feel the same at that depth the next, even if you are acclimatised. Other factors affect your response – stress, fatigue, dehydration, weather – and it is very important to plan deep dives very precisely so that every factor is working in your favour.

One of the deepest dives done on ordinary compressed air was that of Bret Gilliam in 1990, who reached the astonishing depth of 140 metres (over 450 feet). During the few moments he spent at that depth he was able to complete a few simple arithmetical problems, and sign his name on the calculation board. His was the extreme limit of acclimatisation; in the year preceding the dive he never had more than a six-day break from diving, and made 627 dives, including 103 to below 90 metres (300 feet). He also had a personal physiology that allowed him to achieve the dive. The current air depth record holder is Dr Dan Manion, who passed out at approximately 500ft while bringing his descent to a halt, and regained consciousness on his way back to the surface. Most of us would succumb to the effects of depth before we were half-way there, and, in the words of one committed technical diver, such record seeking is like "... setting the Bonneville Salt Flats speed record while drunk ... what's the point?".

There are factors that will pre-dispose almost any diver to the effects of nitrogen narcosis, they are:

- Low temperature
- Stress and anxiety
- Alcohol abuse (hangover)
- Drugs
- Heavy workload and high CO_2 levels
- Fatigue
- Speed of compression (descent rate)
- Poor physical condition

The solutions to most factors on this list are obvious, as most of the problems are self-induced. Many of the predisposing factors, such as fatigue, high workload, alcohol abuse (which contibutes to dehydration) and anxiety can also be predisposing factors to decompression illness. The message is simple – stay healthy! Avoid drinking alcohol the night before, sleep well before diving, do not work too hard underwater, stay warm and do not get stressed. Remember that drugs include nicotine and caffeine – the latter is a diuretic and can contribute to dehydration, as in fact can many fruit juices. Hydrate well before a dive but avoid tea or coffee before a deep dive, and stick to apple juice, water or isotonic drinks. If you are regularly using enriched nitrox mixtures, remember that a switch back to air can be a switch back to narcosis levels you may have become unacclimatised to.

Above all, try and stay fit! Too many divers go deep when their level of personal fitness is far from suitable for such a journey. Such behaviour is neither brave nor sensible, simply stupid. If you want to dive deep, maintain a reasonable level of fitness.

Modern diving equipment – drysuits, thermal underwear, high-performance regulators and ancillary equipment can mean that the effects of narcosis are comparatively less for a well-equipped and rested diver than for a stressed diver with poor equipment. If you must go deep, get fit, train properly, and buy appropriate equipment!

Oxygen toxicity

Whilst most divers are familiar with narcosis, it is less well known that oxygen itself is toxic at depth. This is because as depth increases, so does the pressure of the gas you are breathing, and thus of all the constituent parts of the gas. Too high a partial pressure of oxygen can eventually set off a pulmonary (whole body) reaction, with fluid build-up in the lungs and associated respiratory failure. Though this is a longer term effect, and does not influence the diver during the course of a single dive, it is a cumulative problem and must be allowed for. A more immediate threat, at higher partial pressures, is an immediate toxic reaction – leading quickly to convulsions, the symptoms being identical to an underwater version of an epileptic fit.

Pure oxygen is generally accepted to reach its acceptable toxicity levels at a partial pressure of 1.6 bar. The depth equivalent of this is 6 metres. You should NEVER breathe pure oxygen in the water beyond this depth. Remember, toxicity is time-dependent, and can occur at lower partial pressures when breathed for long enough. The table below shows the time limits imposed on nitrox divers for in-water periods at particular partial pressures. This is examined in greater detail in the chapter on Nitrox later in this volume.

The accepted in-water limit for oxygen partial pressures is 1.6 bars, for a maximum bottom time of 45 minutes. If you are breathing air (which contains 21% oxygen), you reach this partial pressure at 66 metres. This is effectively the limit imposed on deep diving on air by simple virtue of its oxygen content, even if you are extremely tolerant to narcosis,. Beyond 66 metres, the very air you are breathing is toxic. Experienced deep divers, whatever gas mixture they are using, will aim to limit the oxygen partial pressure on the "bottom" to no more than 1.4 or 1.5. This both reduces the potential for oxygen poisoning and allows oxygen-enriched air to be used during the decompression phase of the dive.

To be truthful, the moment you take a cylinder full of compressed air into the water it becomes a nitrox mixture that simply has a partial pressure of 0.21 bar at the surface. At 10 metres it is nitrox with a partial pressure of 0.42 bar, and so on. It would be reasonable to assume that air is an acceptable gas mixture to breathe from 0-60 metres, though not perhaps the best. There are, as we will see, gas mixtures that make diving in the shallower end of that range even safer.

NOAA NITROX TIME LIMITS (mins.)

PPO_2	Single exposure time	Daily maximum
1.6	45	150
1.5	120	180
1.4	150	180
1.3	180	210
1.2	210	240
1.1	240	270
1.0	300	300
0.9	360	360
0.8	450	450
0.7	570	570
0.6	720	720

Carbon dioxide (CO_2) blackout

As you breathe any diving gas mixture, be it air, nitrox, trimix or heliox, one of the gases produced and accumulated within your body is carbon dioxide. This is normally exhaled into the environment, where various natural reactions take care of it. It is not designed to be recycled into your body. Any build-up of CO_2 within your breathing cycle is extremely dangerous.

Carbon dioxide can build up within a breathing cycle in one of several ways. In full-face masks, or while using any system that contains a potential "dead-space" between your mouth and the exhaust valve, CO_2 can accumulate within that space and be re-inhaled. Levels of as little as 0.05 bar are toxic, more than 0.1 bar is lethal.

An inefficient regulator (causing breathlessness and panting at depth), or restrictive clothing or harnesses, or improper use of a free-flow helmet or full-face mask, or an inefficient or exhausted CO_2 scrubber in a rebreather are all ways in which CO_2 build-up can occur. All of these have obvious solutions.

The final, and most insidious, way in which CO_2 can accumulate is within your lungs themselves, simply by not exhaling fully, or by not breathing properly. Rapid, shallow breathing or panting, or breath-holding, can result in dangerous levels of CO_2 building up in your system. The result is black-out, often without much warning, and probable death by drowning or asphyxia.

CO_2 retention can be slightly more prevalent at higher partial pressures of oxygen – such as those found when breathing enriched nitrox or air at depth. This may be because the higher oxygen levels reduce the breathing reflex slightly, allowing the CO_2 to accumulate more readily in your system. CO_2 is a vaso-dilator – it encourages blood-flow by widening the blood vessels, thus increasing the flow of dissolved gases to the brain and the body tissues. The effects of all dissolved gases may be more pronounced, and high CO_2 levels also predispose a diver to oxygen poisoning.

As CO_2 levels rise they cause an increase in the rate and depth of breathing (hypercapnia). If this rise continues, a headache will occur and breathlessness will increase, leading to confusion and a loss of consciousness in extreme cases. Be alert for these signals!

If you do feel CO_2 poisoning is affecting you, then take the following actions immediately. Stop any physical exertion. Get in a stable position, and relax as much as possible. Stay calm. Concentrate on regaining a controlled breathing rate. Flush your system with air by taking deep, controlled breaths, or by flushing a full face-mask or helmet. Do not try to communicate until you regain a stable breathing rhythm. If your regulator is inefficient, try to take long, slow, deep breaths – avoid sucking. If you are on a closed or semi-closed system where the CO_2 absorbent is exhausted, switch to an open circuit system as soon as possible. If the situation demands, leave the water as soon as you can.

The main answer to CO_2 retention is simply to make sure you have adequate equipment, and breathe properly. Do not skip-breathe, do not pant, but breathe in a deep and regular rhythm. Avoid getting stressed – stressed breathing rhythms lead inevitably to potential CO_2 poisoning. If you do want to make your gas supply last longer, get yourself in the best physical shape you can, and practice slow, rhythmic breathing in a pool. You might also think about carrying more gas in the first place!

Decompression

Decompression is regarded as the bogeyman of sport diving. All sport diving organisations recommend that it is avoided, and so it has gathered a mythos about it that is not entirely deserved. Decompression is the application of a series of a mathematical algorithm that calculates the pressurised gas loading acquired by the human body following any dive which is long or deep enough to make slow depressurisation necessary. Put simply, it's a question of hanging round a few metres below the surface for long enough to get rid of the bubbles of inert gas you've gained at depth. While a proper understanding of the physiological processes involved is necessary for the safe practice of decompression diving on a regular basis, it's safer and a lot easier than getting rid of a hangover, which, equally self-induced and in many

DECOMPRESSION TABLES

Italian,
US Navy and derivatives
  (eg. PADI, NAUI)
BSAC 88 (Hennessy)
Bühlmann (Swiss) (various models)
DCIEM (Canadian)

cases more frequently, is far worse for you than the occasional planned bout of decompression.

Most sport diving organisations have agreed that there is really no such thing as a no-decompression dive. There is now a general recommendation that you spend a few minutes at 3 or 6 metres at the end of your ascent following any dive greater than 10 metres. This is called a "safety stop". There are any number of applied decompression tables that make more precise calculations on decompression based on the length of time it takes for various types of body tissue (fat, blood, muscle, bone, etc) to lose the inert gas taken up under the pressure of various depths and the passing of various periods of time. These theoretical tissue types are known as tissue compartments, and reflect the different densities of the range of tissues involved and their rate of inert gas uptake via arterial and capilliary distribution. Muscle, for example, has one of the fastest rates of gas absorption and release, due to the extensive capillary beds within it. Fat, on the other hand, has fewer capillaries and a poorer circulatory network, and therefore both accumulates and releases dissolved gas more slowly.

Some decompression tables are more "conservative" than others. Some are based on more tissue compartments, which is felt to make them safer, others take into account the effect of gas still dissolved in the tissues from previous dives. It is perhaps better to regard such tables as "safer" rather than "more conservative", and it seems sensible to use a set of tables that is more applicable to your physical condition, age, and state of health, the workload you are undertaking and the physical parameters posed by the water you are diving in (eg, current, temperature, visibility). The less fit you are, the older you are, the greater the stresses posed by the work and physical environment you are in, then the more "conservative" your choice of decompression tables should be. The main reason for using a set of decompression tables is, after all, to emerge from the water unbent, rather than in the shortest possible time. The list of most commonly used tables is given in a generally agreed order, with the most conservative at the bottom. Almost all are based on the original work of Professor J.S.Haldane in the early part of the century, and could thus be termed Neo-Haldanian or Modified Haldanean tables.

Most modern decompression computers use one of the Bühlmann algorithm variations for working out decompression schedules, with a smattering basing their calculations on the US Navy or DCIEM tables. The table below lists some of the popular makes of computer and the tables they are based on.

There are a few computer software systems around which allow more accurate dive planning, or which allow for the generation of special decompression tables based on different gas mixtures, gas switches or multiple profiles. Most of these, like the DCAP programme, are too expensive and perhaps too complex for the average sport diver, but others, like the Abyss (various algorithns), are less expensive and readily available. The user should be very aware of the physiological problems of decompression and gas absorbtion on the human body, and should be very careful when using provocative programmes (eg, multi-level dives, multiple ascents) with such s system. Multiple ascents can, for example, lead to a greater disposition to CNS Decompression Illness (central nervous system) and simply because the programme says a dive can physically be done does not mean that it is physiologically safe to do it. Remember that much of this is applied numer-

TABLES USED BY
DECOMPRESSION COMPUTERS

Computer	Table	Number of Compartments
Scubapro DC-11	Bühlmann-Hahn P5	6
Aqualung Monitor 2	Bühlmann ZHL-16	6
Aladin Pro	Bühlmann ZHL-16	6
Micro-Brain Pro	Bühlmann-Hahn P4	6
Parkway Legend	Bühlmann ZHL-16	6
Suunto Solution	Nikkola SME	
Seiko Bridge	Bühlmann	6
Orca	Modified Haldanean	12

ology rather than applied physiology, and that we need both disciplines to be present to provide safe diving.

There are a variety of algorithms derived from the original Bühlmann algorithm, which take into account such factors as bounce diving, rapid ascents, multiple ascents and repeated diving in a single day. A set of tables which appears more conservative is not necessarily a table for "wimps". As more is known about the effects of decompression diving, especially on the problems of multiple repeat dives and varied ascent rates, the move is towards a greater degree of caution, for good reason. Remember, a more "conservative" table is a safer table.

Decompression Illness is usually thought of as having two stages. There is the short term stage, the immediate and short term clinical symptoms (see Chapter 7) which can be treated by recompression therapy. Then there is the second stage, the possible long term effects, which may at best be capillary damage and change in the retina, and at worst ranges from paralysis or brain lesions to death. Getting bent can be more than a pain, and anything that helps avoid permanent, long term damage is worth considering. A few minutes of extra decompression, or a more conservative set of tables, or safer gas mixtures, are worth every bit of time and effort spent on them. Mankind's original design specifications did not include pre-adaption to high pressure environments.To exceed those specifications is to require that the revised limits still support life.

Gas consumption

Put simply, as depth and pressure increase, the rate at which your breathing gas is consumed will also increase. You inspire gas at the same partial pressure as the water around you, and this means, for example, that at 2 bar (10 metres) you consume gas twice as rapidly as at the surface, and at 5 bar (40 metres) you consume it five times as fast. The deeper you go, the more gas you will have to take with you to be safe.

With an open circuit SCUBA system, there is little you can do about gas consumption rates other than by learning through practice and experience to regulate your breathing rhythm so that you consume an adequate supply of gas without inducing CO_2 poisoning and without transcending the amounts your body needs to survive. Do not skip-breathe, and do not hyperventilate, but find a happy and comfortable medium in between. Once you've reached that position, take note of how much gas you require at a particular depth for a particular period, and base your calculations for future dives on that, taking into account such variables as temperature, workload and physical health. As a guideline, average gas consumtion at the surface is between 10-30 litres per minute, depending on workrate (see Chapter 5).

You will consume less gas if you are not unduly stressed in any way. You will consume less gas if you are warm and comfortable, and if your regulator is properly adjusted and suitable for the dive you are doing. Keep your workload to a reasonable level, and develop techniques to cope with environmental hazards such as currents in as relaxed a manner as possible. If you are going really deep, or on a deep training dive, do not plan any work at all.

The easiest way to increase the availability of breathing gas is to simply take more with you, either in larger cylinders or in extra ones (stage diving). Never be afraid of surfacing with a large amount of gas still in your tanks – it is better that than the opposite!

The diving reflex

The diving reflex is a cardio-vascular response to going underwater. It induces a number of body changes – your pulse rate drops, sometimes by as much as half, and the blood vessels reduce their flow to the extremities, diverting heat to the body core. It shares some of the syms of hypothermia without necessarily sharing the reduced mental perception of your surroundings. Marine mammals, like seals, whales and dolphins have the diving reflex to a much greater degree, and can also use it to ward off the effects of low oxygen levels or to increase breath-holding time, which man cannot. The effects on humans are, at best, poorly understood, but the diving reflex does exist, and it does affect your physiology when you enter the water.

The diving reflex does help us to adapt our body's performance to short term in-water periods, when we are properly aware of its existence. Allowing a few moments of adjustment at the beginning of each dive, simply immersing the face in water whilst breathing through the mouth (bradycardial breathing), triggers a slowing of heart and breathing rate that enables properly prepared and low-stressed divers to make better use of their gas supplies by acclimatising themselves before proceeding to depth.

On the down side, in extreme cases of normal low heart rate or abnormal heart rhythms, it can result in blackout or death, especially in older males and in colder water, where breathing rates may also be affected. The rate of immersion also contributes – as the body enters the water and the pressure on it increases, there is an increase in "venous return", the blood flow back to the heart. When venous return occurs, the heart rate also drops since the body likes to keep the amount of blood flow constant.

Buoyancy

By now you should be realising that most of the problems associated with depth are inter-related. Narcosis can be reduced by reducing stress, which also affects decompression and gas consumption, all of which are affected by temperature and workload, etc. Buoyancy is no exception. If you are able

A double "wings" BC setup suitable for deep diving use in combination with a drysuit.

to maintain proper buoyancy throughout your dive, ideally as second nature, then your gas consumption will improve, stress levels will decrease, workload may be reduced and your breathing rate will be more even.

As noted earlier, deep diving requires that two forms of buoyancy control be available on every deep dive. One of these can be a drysuit, and one should be some form of buoyancy compensator with a lift volume capable of raising you, the diver, with either full or almost-empty cylinders, full weight-belt, and possibly a flooded drysuit, to the surface. Ideally it should be able to lift you and your companion as well in an emergency. Do not be tempted to buy a BC because it is close-fitting and pretty – think why you need it in the first place, and look for volume and design efficiency. You need, for deep diving, at least 20-25kg of primary lift in your BC.

For overhead environment diving (wreck, cave or ice), a BC with a dual bag construction is advisable, where the outer protective bag offers some added protection from puncture and abrasion. Do not inflate your drysuit AND your BC from the same cylinder, but make sure that they have separate sources of inflation gas (note that this does not include emergency CO_2 capsules or small emergency air cylinders). If you must dive on a single cylinder, use a small pony bottle to inflate your secondary inflation device and your main cylinder to inflate your primary one. If your pony bottle is also your emergency breathing reserve, do not use your secondary inflation device other than in an emergency (and really consider whether a pony bottle is sufficient).

If you are using a wetsuit, your choice of buoyancy compensators is more limited. There are few BCs on the market which offer a level of redundancy, other than the "wings" system, where the BC is a back-mounted, wing-type pack which offers the possibility of back-to-back duplication. Alternatively, a small wings BC can be doubled with a standard vest-type BC without being unduly unwieldy. Again, each should be filled from an entirely separate source. Using a standard horse-collar BC (or ABLJ) with any other system, even Wings, involves a lot of straps and potential confusion, and is not recommended for technical diving.

ALWAYS HAVE TWO SEPARATE FORMS OF BUOYANCY CONTROL

Temperature

Temperature is the most controllable of the several environmental factors that can affect deep diving. While there is little that can be done about currents or low visibility, if the water is cold you can still keep warm. Make sure the wet or drysuit you are using is appropriate to the dive you are planning, and make sure you are as warm as possible before you enter the water. Cold is a predisposing factor to both narcosis and decompression illness, and enhances stress. You will also breathe more gas.

Conversely, when leaving the water, be careful of warming up too quickly. Leaping straight into a hot bath or shower, or even worse, into a sauna, is to invite a bends hit. If you are hypothermic, it is the worst thing you could do, because it takes blood from the body core, where it is most needed, and carries it rapidly to your extremities.

After a couple of hours in the water, your system has removed the equivalent of a pint of blood from your circulation into your bladder, because your body has been buoyantly suspended and your heart does not need to pump so hard to get blood from head to toe. The shock of too rapid a redistribution of blood flow can cause loss of consciousness or, in bad cases, of in-water hypothermia, even death. When you surface it is better to get out of the wind, somewhere reasonably warm, and have a hot drink. Leave the shower or bath for an hour or so and you will stand far less chance of turning sub-clinical DCI into clinical symptoms, and you will give your system less of a shock.

Chemical heating packs, available from various sources, can be used to keep parts of the body warm on extended dives, though care should be taken to try them out in a controlled environment first. Divers have been burned by strapping such packs next to the skin and using them for the first time on long decompressions, where little can be done about the side effects until the surface has been reached. Wearing such packs outside gloves or above undersuits, may be more appropriate. Remember also that when their heating ability has run out they become little ice packs next to your skin. Use them appropriately, or not at all.

Urination

The loss of blood due to buoyant suspension, as mentioned above, is one of the reasons divers feel the need to pee after spending an hour or so in the water (relief of nervous tension being the other). While replacement of body fluids by taking plenty of water or isotonic drinks is essential, so may be the provision of some kind of facility to catch the end product. Some drysuits (notably the DUI range) can be fitted with catheter attachments that allow the diver to pee directly into the water via a condom like device or a close-fitting sanitary cup, but it may be more convenient for those who do not wish (or fear to rely) on such equipment to use large nappies of the type available for adult incontinence. These have been used by rig divers for many years, and work reasonably well, though some degree of control is needed to urinate slowly enough to allow the material time to absorb the flow. Leakage is both unpleasant, unhealthy and, after a while, simply cold. Even good drysuits do not work as well as would a good wetsuit with fluid slopping around inside , and there is a thermal as well as a comfort disadvantage in not coping properly with spilt urine.

Equally, urine retention over long periods can be extremely dangerous, leading to renal reflux, and must be avoided. Do not allow shyness or incaution to compromise safety, and, if you think you will be in the water for a long time, take due precautions to avoid the unpleasantness that may otherwise occur.

Long-term effects of deep diving

As mentioned previously, there are some potential effects of long-term deep diving that you should be aware of. Some are decompression-related, especially if you have been bent, and these include brain lesions, or muscle and nerve damage which may be permanent. The greater the severity of a bends hit, the more severe the long term effects can be.

What is less known is that, even without experiencing clinical decompression illness, deep diving can have long term effects on your physiology. Post-mortem analyses of the spinal columns of some divers who have a history of deep diving, even with no decompression-related illnesses, have shown nerve and tissue damage that may have affected their health. A change in the pattern of capillaries in the retina is often visible in regular deep divers, though there is no evidence to say that this damages eyesight, other than, in some cases, by a possible slight loss of peripheral vision.

This retinal change, caused by capillary die-off, probably mirrors affects

Decompressing after a deep dive.

to body parts other than the eye, such as the brain, bones and liver. The long term results of such capillary die-off and associated bodily change are poorly understood at present. Aseptic bone necrosis, which typically affects the ends of long bones, is a disease more commonly seen in caisson workers and saturation divers, who spend long periods under pressure. Some modern research indicates it may be a function of too rapid compression rather than decompression. Different tissues in the body compress at different rates, and tissues within the blood which compress more slowly than the surrounding vessels may end up blocking the finest of capillaries before compression is complete.

What has been realised is that the rate of both compression (descent) and decompression (ascent) are crucial to physiological well-being. Slower ascent rates, typically 10 metres/minute, have become the norm, and there is a move towards slower descent rates, of between 10 and 20 metres/minute, to allow various tissue types to compress in a less stressful and more even manner. If, as suspected, many diving diseases are compression-related as well, then taking your time on descent instead of heading down as rapidly as you can, may work in your favour in the long term.

When, eventually, most deep diving is carried out using rebreathers and heliox mixtures, some of these problems should be alleviated. For diving purposes, helium is a much more suitable component of breathing gas than nitrogen, and it appears to have fewer of the long term physiological side effects.

Planning a deep dive

In technical diving, dive planning takes a far higher priority than in ordinary recreational diving. It matters more what you do, and precisely how you do it. There are additional problems of gas mixture planning, decompression schedules, equipment requirements, and the personal demands of the team to consider. Planning takes on a much more operational profile, rather than a vague awareness of roughly what the others in the water plan to do, and where approximately they are going. Technical divers need to be much more precise and aware of the need to follow exact procedures at every point of the dive.

The team

No-one should undertake a deep dive (over 40 metres) who is not already an experienced shallow water diver. It is unfair to subject an inexperienced diver to the additional stresses of deep diving or decompression diving unless he or she has already mastered the basic skills of underwater survival.

Any dive involving the training of previously experienced divers in deep diving techniques should have simply that as its sole purpose. You should not mix basic training in deep diving techniques with any form of work or exploratory dive. The trainee divers have enough on their plate simply being there at depth, and coping with the new techniques and sensations. Too often there is a tendency for more experienced divers to want to show off their skills to those less experienced than themselves. If you feel you are being taught by someone like this, change instructors!

When undertaking a deep dive for reasons other than training try whenever possible to pick someone with a similar level of experience and skill to yourself. Remember that almost every deep dive is virtually a solo dive – you should not be there unless you are capable of getting yourself out of any potential emergency and safely back to the surface. Your buddy is there for company and possible assistance, not as an essential life-saver. If you mix divers with levels of experience that are too far apart, then with the best will in the world you risk:

a)   the inexperienced diver getting into trouble by not wishing to seem incapable, and

b)   the experienced diver forgetting just how hard it was to do things when inexperienced.

It is extremely difficult for one diver to understand the weaknesses of another, unless you have an extremely good and very empathetic individual as a buddy. Most of us are usually lacking a little in that department.

If levels of experience are high, the conditions allow, and the team members are compatible, then there may be something to be said for a group of three diving together where each is practised in solo diving, and diving with a redundant setup. Sometimes it is easier for two divers to take turns to help a third in distress than for one diver to help another alone.

Do make sure, if you are relying to any degree on another diver to support you, that you are both aware of each other's needs and that you each understand

Pre-dive equipment checks are vital.

the other's equipment. Look while you're checking each other's gear to see where an emergency mouthpiece is kept, agree on which side you will swim if in distress, examine cylinder valves so you will know how and where to turn them on and off, and make sure your buddy is happy that he or she is equally comfortable with your equipment.

Briefings

Make sure your team understands exactly what the dive plan is, and that no-one should deviate from it unless an emergency occurs. Make sure that any necessary changes are communicated to everyone, whether they happen before the dive or in the water. Agree on decompression schedules and bottom times, and make sure that everyone is fit and well, with adequate equipment and an adequate gas supply to complete the planned dive safely. Make sure that everyone understands how to operate all the equipment being used, and run through the emergency procedures while still on land.

Most things that are likely to go wrong on any particular dive can be anticipated. Some are common to all dives – such as running out of air or losing a weightbelt. Some are specific to the particular dive – such as losing a guideline, dropping a special tool or stage cylinder, being swept from a decompression line by currents, and so on. Predict every problem and examine all possible solutions. Then, if something does go wrong, you have an indication of how to react, and are more likely to do so in an effective time frame. If you cannot anticipate how to solve a particular problem, avoid it by cancelling or restructuring the dive. Do make sure that everyone is aware of how to solve these problems; a proper dive briefing should cover all of this.

In-water planning

Down lines

When planning a deep dive, there are a few cardinal guidelines that should be followed. Make sure you always have contact with the surface by using a down-line anchored firmly to the bottom and to the boat or surface above. This should be thick and strong enough to pull on if necessary. Remember that a good down-line also helps you to maintain a regular and controlled rate of ascent. From that down-line, it is useful, and probably essential, to run a guideline where visibility is low or currents are strong. If your down-line is also the anchor line, it is even more essential to run a guideline to maintain contact with the boat in case the anchor drags free. All divers should either maintain contact with the guideline in low visibility, or keep it in visual contact in good visibility, and no more than three divers should use any one guideline. Should you get entangled in it, do not cut yourself free until everyone on the line is on the "up" side. (see Chapter 6 for information on line laying and handling).

If you are carrying stage cylinders, and need to remove them, keep them firmly attached to the down-line or guideline. Better still, keep them with you if practical. Make sure any stage cylinder you carry has the contents and mixture clearly marked on it, and that it is easily identifiable as yours (by attaching a label, or painting your name on it).

Decompression lines

Where decompression stops are necessary, do avoid having more than three people decompressing at the same stop on any one line. Trying to

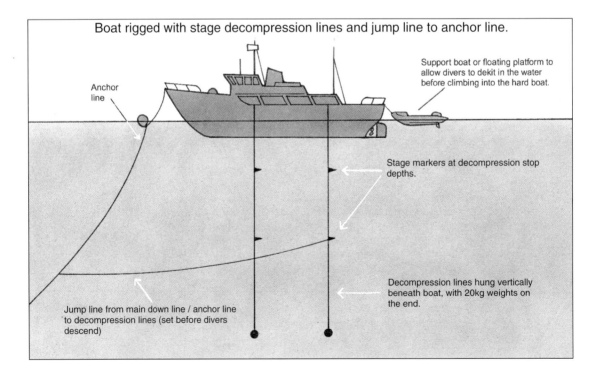

Boat rigged with stage decompression lines and jump line to anchor line.

Support boat or floating platform to allow divers to dekit in the water before climbing into the hard boat.

Anchor line

Stage markers at decompression stop depths.

Decompression lines hung vertically beneath boat, with 20kg weights on the end.

Jump line from main down line / anchor line to decompression lines (set before divers descend)

maintain station in calm water is difficult enough, but when several people are trying to share one small area of sea, clashing gear against each other and becoming entangled in each other's equipment, it is a recipe for disaster.

Hang several decompression lines from your boat, or the surface, to a distance to 10 metres beyond the first predicted stop (for safety's sake). Link these to the main down-line by jump lines, perhaps marked by coloured arrows or name tags to separate them. This allows groups of divers to decompress at the same time without interfering with each other's space.

Line reels can be used to hang back horizontally from a cluster of divers, giving an individual diver more space, but this can be awkward in low visibility, offering potential for entanglement. A decompression sling, or a short piece of rope with a climbing ascender on the end, may be useful for maintaining position while keeping your hands free, especially in a strong current. Alternatively, a line fastened to your harness, with a clip that can be hooked into a loop tied at the stop depth on the decompression rope, can serve the same purpose, acting as a safety link in case the current sweeps you from the decompression line.

Once all divers are safely attached to the decompression lines, it may, depending on sea conditions and currents, be prudent to detach the dive vessel from the anchor line (buoy it first!) or raise anchor and let the vessel drift with the flow. This will

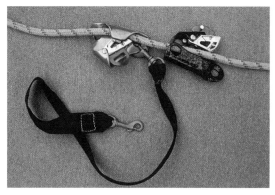

make decompression much more comfortable for those below, reducing stress and work load in strong currents. Do work out just how far the boat will travel during the anticipated decompression time, and beware of rocks, shipping lanes or other obstacles that may be encountered en route.

Top: Decompression lines from the boat. Above: Personal decompression sling.

Stage decompression

If different gas mixtures are being used during decompression (nitrox, oxygen, etc.), do make sure everyone is changing at the right places. Check each other's regulator switches at the appropriate stops, and time any air-breaks that may be required (see use of oxygen below).

Never rely on decompression cylinders left in place on down lines or shotlines at the start of the dive. If the boat breaks anchor while you are down, they may not be there when you get back. It's no fun floating in the middle of the sea with missed decompression. Try and carry your decompression gas with you at all times. By all means leave safety cylinders on shotlines below the boat, equipped with with multiple regulators or octopus rigs, or even via surface-supplied umbilicals, but regard those as spare supplies, not as your main source of decompression gas.

When diving in strong currents – and really on all deep dives – you should take with you an emergency marker buoy and a small reel with enough line to reach the surface from at least 20 metres

ALWAYS CARRY ALL YOUR DECOMPRESSION GAS

Right: Decompression buoy and float.

below your first planned stop. If you drift off the site, this is the only way you may have of letting those at the surface know. Let the buoy go towards the surface when you reach a depth shallower than the length of line on your reel, though not with enough positive buoyancy to drag you uncontrollably with it, and rise to your first decompression stop, keeping the line taut between you and the buoy . Allow yourself to drift with the current, and keep the buoy inflated when you reach the surface. Once all the others have decompressed and boarded, the boat should be able to find you by following the direction of the current until it reaches you.

On all decompression dives, try and keep your workload as light as possible during decompression. High-stress or hard work decompressions are not a good idea, and can lead to your getting bent. Use your decompression sling to allow yourself to hang freely without effort, and avoid strong currents wherever possible.

Free-hang decompression

There are several methods by which decompression can be made away from a shotline, either free-hanging in the water, or by letting a line up from the seabed or a wreck.

The latter is a straightforward way by which divers may explore more on a dive than would be possible if they had to return to a downline, especially against a current. The diver carries a reel which contains enough line to reach the surface, plus 50% to allow for being swept sideways by any current which may be present. The line is attached to a secure belay on the bottom, and is unwound as the diver ascends.

When using such a line the effects of swell during decompression are negligible, and a surface marker buoy can be sent to the surface during stops to indicate the divers' position. If hemp line, which rots quickly, is used it can be cut and left on completing decompression. If a nylon or synthetic fibre line is used, then it should be doubled so that it can be pulled back to the surface once decompression is complete. In the latter case, tie a short tape sling to the bottom and pass the doubled line through this, or pass the line through a disposable snap-link.

If you are carrying out free-hanging decompression, either by intent or accident, make contact with the surface as soon as practicable. The divers should ascend to the first decompression stop and let up a decompression buoy to signal their presence to the surface cover. The buoy can be attached either to a line reel, which must contain enough line to reach the surface from the first stop, and which can be reeled in as the diver ascends, or it can be attached to a drop weight on the end of a tape or cord which is itself longer than the depth of the decompression stops. The correct technique for using this method is: first, on arrival at the decompression stop the divers adjust their buoyancy, they then drop the weight and its line while retaining the decompression buoy, when the line is fully deployed they inflate the buoy and let it rise to the surface, they can then decompress on the line hanging from the buoy.

The best type of buoy for free-floating decompression is one which has 10-20 kg of lift and which is fitted with an auto-inflation device. This can support one or two divers hanging below it and can reduce the stress of suspension in the swell. A short length of shock-cord just below the decompression buoy will help absorb some of the effects of swell. This can be backed up by a length of safety line to avoid the possibility of breakage.

Whatever method is used, take care to ensure that the buoy can ascend freely on the decompression line without any possibility of dragging the diver up with it in an uncontrolled ascent. It is perhaps unwise to use a reel with an automatic locking device if there is any possibility of it being dragged from the diver's hand. A reel without such a device will fall freely below the buoy and can be recovered.With such a device there is a risk that it may float away beyond the reach of the diver if it pulls free while being deployed.

Line reels

A good line reel should be simple to use and have the following features. It should have a handle, or be otherwise easy to hold during deployment, It should have an uncomplicated method of winding the line back in with some type of positive line-locking device. It should have a line guide to avoid spillage and a clip to attach it to the diver when not in use. Several types of line reel, such as those shown on pages 73 and 74, can be readily home-made. If you decide to make your own reels, take care to make them correctly. Your life can depend on the correct functioning of a reel, and badly-made reels have a habit of falling apart underwater, spilling coils of loose line in which it is only too easy for you or another diver to become entangled. If you do spill line, try to recover it if it is safe to do so. If the line is badly tangled it may be easier to use a small stuff bag instead of the reel.

When storing line on a reel remember that wet line can be bulkier than dry line, so do not over-fill the reel. You could find that you have too much line to fit on the reel when winding it back in underwater.

Beware of expending too much energy getting back in the boat.

Recovery to a boat or the surface

Following any decompression, it is essential to avoid unnecessary physical effort during the immediate post-surfacing period. One or two divers should be delegated as surface-cover/in-water assistant on such dives, to stay in the boat until divers start surfacing. People get bent by hauling large cylinders and themselves out of the water and up the ladder. Whenever possible, take all your gear off in the water (get someone to help you) and either pass it up to those on the boat, or clip it to a line and haul it in later. Once you are out of the water, sit down for a minute or two and

KEEP EFFORT AFTER SURFACING TO A MINIMUM

relax. Replace body fluids with isotonic drinks as soon as you can. Once you are rested and your pulse and breathing have returned to normal, haul your gear carefully in and strip it down as slowly and calmly as possible.

If nothing else, you will avoid the "post-dive syndrome", the niggling headache and general feeling of malaise caused by sub-clinical decompression illness, where lots of tiny bubbles are buzzing round your bloodstream due to that final pressure gradient being abused. It is a warning that you're just shy of being clinically bent.

Deep ocean dives

On deep open-water dives, where the boat cannot anchor, it is essential to either keep it in sight at all times or, preferably, to be physically linked to it. Wind and surface currents may carry it from you faster than you can swim. If you are concerned about large marine mammals, consider hanging some form of refuge, like a shark cage, at your longest decompression stop, or on a winch where it can be hauled from stop to stop.

Oxygen decompression

Many deep divers regularly – and safely – use pure oxygen at the shallowest decompression stops. Alternatively, oxygen- enriched air, nitrox, can be used, typically with a 40% or 50% oxygen content. Such use of nitrox must be made with due care and attention to a number of details, and only after training in the use and handling of oxygen and nitrox mixtures.

There are several potential risks with this practice, all of which can be easily avoided. Firstly, pure oxygen should NEVER EVER be used below 10 metres, and ideally never below 6 metres. Oxygen (see Chapter 5) should not be breathed in the water at partial pressures in excess of 1.6 bar and then only for periods of up to 45 minutes. Pure oxygen reaches this partial pressure at 6 metres. Make sure that your decompression requirements fit within this figure, and do not, whatever you have heard to the contrary, use pure oxygen arbitarily to reduce the period of decompression stipulated by your tables unless you are working to a proprietary set of tables which compute for this gas change.

PURE OXYGEN SHOULD NEVER EVER BE USED BELOW 6 METRES

Secondly, when using any oxygen mixture which contains more than 40% oxygen, the diving equipment you are using to store it in and breathe it through MUST be oxygen cleaned, painted oxygen green (USA) or black with a white top (UK and Europe), marked OXYGEN and dedicated to oxygen use. (see Chapter 5). Pure or high pressure oxygen, when in contact with certain contaminants (notably hydrocarbons such as oil), can cause a spontaneous explosion. Avoid using pure oxygen with any equipment that is regularly filled with air from an oil-lubricated compressor without first passing the air through adequate filtration to ensure it is compatible with pure oxygen.

OXYGEN DECOMPRESSION CYLINDERS MUST BE IMPOSSIBLE TO BE BREATHED FROM BY MISTAKE AT DEPTH.

More than one diver has died just by doing this. To ensure that this cannnot happen, keep your oxygen cylinder turned off until you reach your 6 metre decompression stop, and place its regulator out of casual reach, either in a pocket or clipped to the side of the cylinder. If necessary, invert the cylinder to ensure that you can easily reach the valve to turn it on when required.

Regulators used with pure oxygen should be clearly colour-coded, ideally with a green medium pressure hose and green markings (integral flashing, insulation tape, etc). A label indicating the regulator is in oxygen service should be attached to it in some way. Contents gauges used with such regulators should be oxygen compatible, and ideally not oil-filled. It is best to use a new gauge with pure oxygen or oxygen-rich mixtures, as one of the most serious points of hydrocarbon accumulation is at the end of the high-pressure hose where it joins the contents gauge. Always assume that an old gauge or hose is contaminated.

By following those simple rules, by keeping equipment oxygen-clean and by not breathing oxygen at too high a partial pressure or to excess, the use of oxygen or oxygen-rich mixtures during decompression offers a greater degree of protection from decompression illness than is gained by simply breathing air at your decompression stops.

As a recommended procedure, it is certainly worth using nitrox for decompression, but it is important to ensure equipment compatibility for the richness of the mix. Where equipment compatibility is in doubt, the schedule can be made safer by simply using a proprietary mixture containing no more than 40% oxygen while decompressing for a full air profile as indicated by a computer or the tables. Nitrox 40 is safe to breathe to a maximum depth of 30 metres (see Chapter 5 for toxicity limits). This itself will certainly provide a significant additional safety factor over air.

Archaeological diver with a Biomarine Mk15 in a Bahamian cave (with skull!).

CHAPTER FIVE

Gas mixtures other than air

IN SPORT DIVING there is a growing recognition that compressed air is a less-than-ideal breathing mixture for divers. At depths over 40 metres it is increasingly narcotic, at medium depths (20-40 metres) is has a considerable decompression penalty, and over 60 metres it becomes downright dangerous. As a breathing mixture, air is at its best between the surface and a depth of 10 metres, and, where the partial pressure of oxygen is concerned, between a depth of 45 and 60 metres (if you don't count narcosis).

Ordinary air is a nitrox mixture containing about 21% oxygen and 79% nitrogen, and a few other trace gases. We were designed by Mother Nature to breathe air at or near sea level, where the partial pressure of oxygen is around 0.21 bar. Our design tolerance is fairly limited, the mixture becomes too weak at partial pressures below 0.16 bar, and too rich above 0.5 bar. As we stray from our 0.21 bar setpoint, the further we drift and the longer we stay, the more out-of-balance our body becomes. It does not take much – unduly long exposures in excess of 0.5 bar of oxygen (the depth equivalent of breathing air at 14 metres) and we develop respiratory problems of a serious nature. We may eventually die. The nitrogen content becomes an increasing problem at partial pressures in excess of 3-4 bar.

We do, however, have the ability, and the design tolerance, to monkey with our breathing mixtures for short periods of time without harm. We can tune our diving gases to increase the oxygen content (and thus decrease the nitrogen content) for fixed time periods, and we can even remove all or part of the nitrogen to further reduce the narcosis problem. All of these practices are safe if carried out properly. Learn the mechanics, and the system can be kept perfectly in tune.

Nitrox

The simplest way to improve the quality of the breathing gas for shallow to medium depth SCUBA diving is to increase the oxygen content of the mix. Oxygen/nitrogen mixtures containing over 22% of oxygen are termed "Enriched Air Nitrox" (EANx). Such nitrox mixtures have been in use in the diving world for decades – they have been used in open and closed circuit equipment by military divers since World War Two, they have been used in recompression and chamber therapy since the 1950s, they have been a part of diving science since the late 1970s, and have been in use in advanced sport diving circles, both as a shallow breathing mixture and a decompression gas, for more than 20 years. We know a lot about nitrox. It's been tried and tested by generations of divers, and it's known to be safer than air as long as a few simple rules are followed.

The main rules concern depth and time exposures. We know that breathing oxygen at partial pressures of over 1.6 bar of the gas in any mixture for more than 45 minutes brings us into what is regarded as the danger zone of oxygen toxicity. That time penalty improves swiftly when we decrease the partial pressure – at 1.5 bar we can spend 120 minutes, at 1.4 bar we can safely spend 150 minutes, and by the time we reach 1 bar, we can spend 5 hours underwater without harm. By adjusting the percentage of oxygen in any nitrox mixture, we can adjust the depth at which we reach a partial pressure of 1.6 bar of the gas. Some of the more common nitrox mixes are listed below, together with their depth limits.

Nitrox Mix	Depth limit at	
	1.6 BAR PPO_2	1.4 BAR PPO_2
EANx 21 (Air – 21%)	66 m	57 m
EANx 28 (28% O_2)	47 m	40 m
EANx 32 (32% O_2)	40 m	35 m
EANx 36 (36% O_2)	34 m	30 m
EANx 40 (40% O_2)	30 m	25 m

The most commonly used recreational nitrox mixtures at the time of writing are 32% and 36% EANx, mixtures which were developed by NOAA (the National Oceanic and Atmospheric Administration) in the USA, back in the 1970s. By using these mixtures, NOAA scientific divers were able to both extend their bottom times and reduce their decompression schedules further than they could when using ordinary compressed air.

The benefits of this nitrox use had a logical knock-on effect. By reducing the nitrogen content of the mix, not only could bottom time be extended and decompression time reduced, but there was correspondingly less narcosis at comparable depths, there was less chance of decompression illness, and, because there was less residual nitrogen in the bloodstream on surfacing, surface intervals could be shorter. More diving could be undertaken during a single day, and it could still be safer diving in the first place! The reduction in residual nitrogen also decreased the "post-dive syndrome". Because there was less nitrogen in the bloodstream, the divers felt better – less exhausted – after the dive, because their circulatory system contained more oxygen and fewer of the sub-clinical bubbles that induced the feeling of lethargy.

As one nitrox convert, an old Maine clam-diver, reputedly put it, "Mah home life has improved tremendously. Ah now feel fresh enough to make love to mah wife at the end o' th' workin' day! Improved her cookin' too!"

The penalty, if penalty there is, for nitrox diving is that of oxygen toxicity. For most sport divers, the diving they would have to do to make this a real problem far exceeds their needs, but for some technical divers, especially those making very long duration dives, often at depth, the penalty is all too real.

Oxygen toxicity is very different from nitrogen toxicity. Nitrogen narcosis can be likened to crashing slowly into a soft cushion – the effects are gradual and insidious as depth increases. You can deal with them, even acclimatise yourself to them, to a degree. Not so oxygen. It's the proverbial brick wall. Crash into oxygen toxicity and the effect can be instantly lethal. Often with little warning, other than muscle twitching or breathing difficulties, or a number of symptoms that bear an unfortunate similarity to nitrogen narcosis, the diver can go cataleptic, then begin convulsing, then lose consciousness. And all too easily die. The convulsions themselves don't kill, and could be easily handled if we were not in the water. But underwater, it's all too easy to lose your mouthpiece and drown.

It's worth pointing out that this can – and has – happened on air. At depths beyond 66 metres, the oxygen partial pressure exceeds 1.6 bar. Very deep air dives, to depths of over 70 metres, bring the diver into a real danger zone, where any increase in effort or a build up of CO_2 in the system can lead quickly to oxygen poisoning. Several "unexplained" deep air diving fatalities in the past few decades were, when looked at from the point of view of oxygen toxicity, suddenly very explicable. Here were divers who had mysteriously died with air still in their cylinders, and regulators in their mouths. What had been regarded as a mysterious malady, "Depth Blackout", was simply oxygen poisoning.

There are a number of things that predispose a diver to oxygen poisoning, such as CO_2 build-up, high work loads, overheating and various contra-indicative drugs, such as Sudafed and other decongestants commonly used by divers. Anything that dilates blood vessels and increases gas transport and tissue absorption is potentially bad news in gas toxicity terms, and should be avoided at all costs. If you are suffering from sino-nasal constriction before a technical dive, abandon the dive. Do not assume that drugs of any sort make it safer.

A good diver will realise that such things are avoidable if planned for. We all drive cars that are capable of breaking speed limits, but most of us recognise that dramatically exceeding these limits places us and others at risk. Life's like that. Too much of anything is bad for us, but that does not mean that everything that is potentially dangerous should be banned. Quite the reverse – if using something properly means that things can be safer, we are duty bound to use it that way.

So it is with nitrox. Use it properly, and it's a safer breathing gas. Use it badly, it's dangerous. By keeping well within the time and depth limits of any nitrox mixture, you can enjoy all the benefits without having to worry about the dangers.

Apart from the obvious physical benefits of a reduced nitrogen mixture in diving, how does nitrox work with decompression times? Simply by using what is called the Equivalent Air Depth concept. Breathing a nitrox mixture at one particular depth can be equated to breathing air at another. All we need to calculate what those depths are is to know the actual depth we will be diving to, and the percentage of oxygen in our nitrox mixture. Breathing EANx 36 (36% oxygen) at 33 metres, for example, gives us an equivalent air depth (EAD) of just 25 metres. So, at 33 metres breathing EANx 36, we have a narcosis equivalent of 25 metres, and can decompress on a 25 metre table. Say we stayed at 33 metres for 30 minutes. Using the Bühlmann tables, on air we would have to decompress for 4 minutes at 6 metres and 11 minutes at 3 metres. On EANx 36, using the 25 metre table, we are still in "no-stop" time, and have only our 1 minute safety stop to make.

The equation used to calculate the Equivalent Air Depth is a simple one :

$$EAD = \frac{(1 - FO_2) \times (D + 10)}{0.79} - 10$$

In this equation, FO_2 is the fraction of oxygen in the mix, expressed as a decimal, and D is the depth of the dive in metres. When working out the example given above, the equation would read like this :

$$EAD = \frac{(1 - 0.36) \times (30 + 10)}{0.79} - 10$$

$$EAD = \frac{0.64 \times 40}{0.79} - 10$$

$$EAD = \frac{25.6}{0.79} - 10$$

$$EAD = 32.4 - 10$$

EAD = 22.4 metres (23 metres)

Using this equation, the equivalent air depths for any nitrox mixture can be calculated, and the result used with any set of decompression tables to re-work the decompression schedule for a single dive. For repeat dives, only decompression tables which allow repeat dives within a single table structure are appropriate (eg, Bühlmann, DCIEM, US Navy and derivatives). The structure of the BSAC'88 tables does not allow nitrox to be used on repetitive dives. Sets of proprietary nitrox tables are available through publications issued by NOAA, DCIEM, TDI, IANTD, and ANDI, which have EAD calculations already made, and which support different percentages of oxygen in the mix.

Another option would be to use a standard air decompression computer as a way of making an irregular profile dive safer. As long as the depth and time limits for the particular nitrox mix are observed, the diver can make his or her computer-generated decompression even safer by using nitrox on the dive and making the full air decompression as required by the computer. For old or overweight divers, or those with some other health problem that might make them susceptible to decompression illness, this is an alternative to be seriously considered. One must remember to calculate the air requirements for the dive, however. With the increased bottom time offered by nitrox, using it with an unknown air decompression can take you into the empty cylinder zone! Always plan such dives with plenty gas in reserve!

Using nitrox in an ordinary 12-15 litre cylinder would probably not give you enough gas at medium depths (15-25 metres) to stay down long enough to reach your no-decompression time. This keeps your dive easily within the safety limits while still giving you longer underwater – and possibly allowing you a second lengthy dive later in the day with no, or minimal, decompression penalty.

Nitrox as a decompression gas

Nitrox mixtures have long been used by deep divers as a decompression gas. While Enriched Air Nitrox in itself is unsuitable as a deep diving gas, its reduced nitrogen content makes it eminently suitable for breathing during decompression stops.

Decompression is all about allowing the dissolved gases in your body tissues enough time to get out without causing you medical problems. By effectively increasing the gradient of diffusion (or, more simply, reducing the amount of nitrogen coming the other way), the dissolved inert gases, whatever they be, can come out of solution more quickly. This is not to say you can necessarily reduce the decompression time – simply that you can improve your chance of not getting bent by doing the full required stop time on a safer breathing mixture. You are giving yourself an extra chance. Deep diving is a risky business, physiologically, and anything that can be done to make it safer is worth doing.

Alternatively, there are custom nitrox tables that allow for a bottom mix of air and an EANx decompression mix. These may be more appropriate where other factors such cold temperatures or physical exposures may make a comparatively longer air decompression more hazardous. Such tables can reduce decompression stops by calculating for the reduced nitrogen loading, but should only be used with a full and proper understanding of the procedures involved, which vary from table to table.

The problems of oxygen toxicity are still there, even on decompression. The PPO_2 limit of 1.6 for 45 minutes must not be exceeded, even during decompression. If nitrox is to be used during stops, and the dive time including decompression exceeds 45 minutes, the diver must not exceed 1.5 bar PPO_2 on the "bottom". (On air dives, this limits the dive to around 60 metres.) If the whole dive lasts less than 120 minutes, the diver can then safely breathe pure oxygen at 3 metres and EANx mixtures containing no more than 1.5 bar $PPO2$ below that depth.

A correctly marked EANx cylinder.

Commonly used decompression gases are Nitrox 40, which reaches 1.5 bar at 28 metres and is therefore safe for all stops above that (and can still be used as a bailout gas), or even Nitrox 60, which reaches 1.5 bar at 15 metres. Note that recommended practices state that any nitrox mixture containing more than 40% oxygen should be treated as pure oxygen, and that all equipment used with it should therefore be both oxygen compatible and oxygen clean (see below).

Training and equipment

No diver should use nitrox in the water unless he or she has been specially trained in its use. Technical Diving International (TDI), The International Association of Nitrox and Technical Divers (IANTD) and American Nitrox Divers Inc. (ANDI) run basic nitrox courses, and a variety of more advanced technical courses in nitrox, mixed gas and deep and overhead environments. Their recommended codes of practice have been developed over many years to make nitrox diving safe, and are worth adhering to. Like deep air diving, using nitrox outside its proper limits is dangerous, and it is worth spending time finding out what these correct limits are.

Cylinders containing EANx mixtures should be marked accordingly. Mistaking them for ordinary compressed air could lead to serious consequences, and both the fact that they contain nitrox, and the actual mix they contain must be displayed. An internationally-recognised colour coding for recreational nitrox SCUBA cylinders is a yellow cylinder with a 10cm wide green band encircling the cylinder just below the neck. The cylinder should be clearly labelled "NITROX", and the percentage of the mix should also be clearly marked. IANTD and TDI both sell adhesive green bands which are already labelled NITROX, and which have space for marking the gas composition and/or the depth to which it can be used. Then all you need is a yellow cylinder on which to stick it! If a cylinder of another colour is used, the green band should have a 2cm yellow immediately above and below it.

We already know that any nitrox mix containing more than 40% oxygen should be regarded as being pure oxygen in equipment compatibility terms, and that equipment used with it should be cleaned and serviced accordingly. This is because pure oxygen, or very oxygen-rich mixtures, become

An oil free compressor with a portable filter stack.

potentially more dangerous at high pressures, and anything that can reduce that risk is beneficial. Oxygen, when in contact with hydrocarbons, can cause spontaneous combustion, and oxygen, whilst not flammable itself, supports combustion robustly. It should NEVER be used near naked flames, and contact with hydrocarbons in any form should be avoided.

When storing pure oxygen, keep it away from heat sources, hydrocarbons and flames, and make sure no-one goes near it with a lighted cigarette. It's another good reason why, if you are a "Technical Diver", you should not smoke!

Nitrox mixtures containing less than 40% oxygen can be safely used with any standard air SCUBA equipment. If you want to use your SCUBA gear with richer mixtures, then all silicon-based components (O-rings, diaphragms, pressure seats) must be replaced with equivalent components made from oxygen compatible materials. If this is not possible then consider using alternative equipment where such parts are compatible with oxygen. All traces of hydrocarbons must be removed, either by cleaning with stabilised trichloroethane or Freon 113 (neither of which are compatible with plastic and are both highly toxic).

Freon 113 is a chlorinated fluorocarbon (CFC), and is extremely damaging to the ozone layer, and is therefore likely to be banned in the near future. Other preferable solvents are available. The best of these, less damaging to the environment, is Citriklene™.

Whatever solvent is used, the general procedure is as follows. Remove all plastic parts and O-rings from regulators, valves, etc, before dipping them. If you must use Freon 113 or 111 trichloroethane, use it sparingly and recycle it (skim the grey deposits off and bottle it well, using a rubber seal) or dispose of it properly. DO NOT just pour it down the drain, it's frighteningly toxic. Alternatively, use Citric acid (clear vinegar is fine – not malt) to remove corrosion, and detergent to remove hydrocarbons. A good detergent, recommended by the US military for oxygen cleaning, is Tribasic Sodium Phosphate, or TSP. Similar to washing powder, this can be purchased under various brand names in hardware stores. Look at the ingredients on the packet before purchasing. Soak metal parts in solvent overnight or clean thoroughly with detergent, rinse well in warm water, and allow to dry properly before reassembling. When equipment is both oxygen clean and oxygen compatible, it is termed to be in "oxygen service".

Do remember that if you use oxygen-service equipment with ordinary, inadequately-filtered compressed air from an oil-lubricated compressor it's no longer oxygen-clean, even if the parts are still oxygen-compatible. To be safe with pure oxygen or hyper- rich oxygen mixtures, equipment must be both oxygen-compatible AND oxygen-clean. This is especially true of nitrox cylinders – keep them for nitrox-dedicated compressors, and make sure that all relevant component parts of the cylinder valve are in oxygen service.

Equally, do not attempt to blend your own nitrox mixtures unless you have undertaken all the required training in mixing and blending procedures, and invested heavily in oxygen service decanting and compressor equipment. Rather, get the appropriate qualification from one of the major nitrox certifying agencies and purchase it from an approved nitrox filling station.

In-water use of oxygen

It has been emphasised repeatedly that all equipment you use for decompression in water with oxygen or hyper-rich nitrox MUST be in oxygen-service. If you plan to use oxygen for the shallowest decompression stops, dedicate a set of equipment to it. Clean and use a cylinder purely for oxygen, and, if possible, use one with a lower working pressure (say around 150 bar). Oxygen is safer at 150 bar than 200 bar. Keep a regulator and gauge in oxygen-service, and use them only with pure oxygen. Make sure the cylinder is painted in oxygen colours (black with a white neck in the UK and Europe, oxygen green in North America) and is clearly marked "Breathing Oxygen". Identify the regulator clearly as in oxygen-service as well, perhaps by winding green insulation tape around the low pressure hose.

An oxygen analyser.

Remember also that the toxicity clock is still ticking away at shallow depths, and keep your oxygen use to below 1.6 bar. Ideally, use pure oxygen only at 3 metres (1.3 bar), unless the whole dive, including decompression, takes less than 45 minutes. Make sure you take an air break every 20-25 minutes, to allow your system some respite, and keep exertion to a minimum. High work rates encourage oxygen toxicity. Do not, for example, plan oxygen decompressions if you are going to be swimming hard into a strong current to maintain position. For most shallow open-circuit decompression, use of a mixture containing between 40 and 80% oxygen is probably safer.

Trimix

In technical diving, trimix is usually taken to be a mixture of oxygen, nitrogen and helium, though technically it is a term used to define a mixture of any three gases to make a breathable diving gas.

Helium is the preferential gas used to further alter nitrox mixtures because it is non-narcotic. By replacing some of the nitrogen with helium, we can reduce the narcotic potential of a breathing mix to bearable proportions.

The main problem with helium is its expense. A cylinder of pure medical oxygen costs about one tenth as much as an equivalent size cylinder of diving grade helium. Bearing in mind that a typical ratio of gases in a technical diving mix is 15/40/45 (O/He/N) then it is obvious that far more helium than oxygen is required for a dive, and most of the oxygen in the mix comes from the air component of the gas. A typical "fill" of trimix – say 2 x 12 litre cylinders, costs about £30-40, when cylinder hire and delivery charges are taken into account. Trimix is not a very cheap option in open circuit equipment, but it does provide a far less narcotic mix at depth. There is no particular depth limit for trimix as a generic gas, the range of diving allowed is, like nitrox, dependent on the partial pressure of the oxygen content and the narcotic potential of the nitrogen present. For different depths, there are different mixes.

Remembering that the percentage of oxygen in air is 21%, and that this reaches the 1.6 bar limit for oxygen partial pressure at 66 metres, then dives below that have to have a reduced percentage of oxygen in order for them to be safe. The mixture quoted above (15/40/45) has an oxygen percentage of 15%, making it safe to depths of almost 100 metres. At the surface, however, its partial pressure is 0.15 bar, making it dangerously hypoxic. To use trimix safely, one must use it in conjunction with a travel mix, an intermediate breathing supply, usually nitrox, that transports you through the low PPO$_2$ zone to a depth at which the trimix is safe to breathe. A Nitrox 36 mix, for example, could transport a diver to 34 metres, at which point the 15% oxygen content of the 15/40 mix has a PPO$_2$ of 0.66 bar, well above the 0.21 bar of air at the surface, but well below the 1.6 bar limit. On this mix, that limit would be reached at 96 metres.

The formulae used to work this out are developed from Dalton's Law (the total pressure of a gas mixture is equal to the sum of the partial pressures of its component gases). The partial pressure of a gas is simply the pressure that constituent gas exerts on the whole ... or the "part" of pressure that gas exerts.

The formula used to find the total pressure of a gas at a given depth is simple (where P = total pressure of the gas in bar.):

P = Depth/10 + 1.

This also allows us to determine depth from pressure, by adjusting the algebra to state that:

Depth(D) = (P – 1) x 10.

For example, the pressure in bar at 30 metres is 30/10 + 1, which is 4 bar. Conversely, the depth at which 4 bar is reached is (4 – 1) x 10 = 30 metres.

The three formulae that have been developed from Dalton's Law that concern mixed gas diving are :

Formula 1: PPg   = Fg x P
Formula 2: Fg   = PPg x P
Formula 3: P   = PPg/Fg

In all of these, **PPg** is the partial pressure of the gas in bar, **Fg** is the fraction of the gas in the mix, expressed as a decimal, and **P** is the total pressure of the gas in bar at depth (gained, remember, from **P = D/10 + 1**).

These formulae can most easily be remembered by using the T-shape below.

$$\frac{PPg}{Fg \mid P}$$

Cover the part of the T to be discovered, and the remainder shows the formula to use (eg, cover **PPg** and you are left with **Fg x P**; cover **P** and you are left with **PPg/Fg**).

In the example above, the depth limit (**P**) at which the mix reaches 1.6 bar PPO_2 was discovered by using **PPg/Fg**, or **PPO_2/FO_2**,

$$\begin{aligned}
\mathbf{PPO_2/FO_2} \quad &= \mathbf{1.6/0.15} \\
&= \mathbf{10.7\ bar}
\end{aligned}$$

Then, using $\mathbf{D = (P - 1) \times 10}$, we get $(10.7 - 1) \times 10$, which gives us our figure of 97 metres.

The formula can be used in advanced nitrox diving to determine the appropriate PPO_2 to use at a particular depth for a particular time, a process that is called "custom blending" a gas mix. For example, to determine the safe oxygen content to use at a depth of 75 metres, we would use: **Fg = PPg/P**. Since we do not want to exceed a PPO_2 of 1.4 bar our formula will read:

Fg $\quad$ **= PPg/P**
(and since 75 m gives 8.5 bar using P = D/10 + 1)
$\qquad$ **= 1.4/8.5**
$\qquad$ **= 0.16**

This gives us our maximum percentage at 80 metres of 16% at 1.4 bar O_2.

Having found the appropriate oxygen content for the trimix, the diver must then calculate just how much narcosis he/she is prepared to accept. This is called calculating the Equivalent Narcosis Depth of the mix. What we are trying to discover is the equivalent nitrogen partial pressure that induces narcosis on air. So, if a diver wishes to experience no more than the narcotic equivalent of a 40 metre dive on air, the PPN_2 of the mix must not exceed that of air at 40 metres, which would be,

using $\mathbf{PPN_2 = FN_2 \times P}$
(and remembering that $\mathbf{P = D/10 + 1}$),
0.79 x 5, or 3.95 bar

On a trimix dive to 75 metres, using the same formulae, the equation would read as:

PPN_2 $\quad$ **= FN_2 x P**
3.95 $\quad$ **= FN_2 x 8.5**

To find the fraction of nitrogen to place in the mix, we would adjust the formula to read:

FN_2 $\quad$ **= PPN_2/P**
$\qquad$ **= 3.95/8.5**
$\qquad$ **= 0.46 bar**

Filling lightweight composite cylinders with trimix, using a Haskel booster pump.

The final mixture would then be adjusted in a similar fashion for the oxygen content, which must never more than 1.6 bar on the bottom, (and ideally no more than 1.4 bar to reduce the potential for oxygen toxicity during lengthy nitrox decompressions). The balance is made up from helium.

To use trimix safely requires special training, and access to special decompression tables. Not only are the gas mixes more sophisticated and dive planning more complex, the environmental exposures generated by diving to depths of up to 100 metres can be immense. In advanced recreational terms, trimix is best suited to the 50 – 80 metre depth range, where a 10 minute dive to 80 metres can create a more acceptable in-water decompression of less than half-an-hour, depending on which tables, mixtures and gas switches are used. In cold water, a more conservative depth of around 75 metres may be more appropriate as a generally recommended limit.

Trimix diving on open circuit scuba is a very serious undertaking, due not only to the complexity of gas management and diving exposures, but to the time limitations for crisis solving at depth. At 80 metres, for example, gas supplies are being consumed 9 times faster than at the surface. A problem-solving crisis lasting five minutes could consume a vast amount of gas. On the same decompression tables that gave 27 minutes of decompression stops for a 10 minute dive, 15 minutes requires 44 minutes, and 20 minutes requires 64 minutes, with all the additional gas requirements for such an extension to the dive.. There is very little room for error, and dive plans have to be absolutely precise, equipment as near perfect as possible, and the number of potential problems that can be coped with reduced to almost zero. Divers who plan using trimix at such depths must be extremely good at coping with stress. Open circuit exposures at these depths are limited by a labyrinthine complex of factors, all of which must be dealt with before, during or after the dive. Mixed gas diving is a much more complicated, and potentially dangerous, business than air or nitrox diving.

It should not be done without considerable experience, preparation and attention to detail.

Heliox

If helium is so good at removing narcosis, why not simply replace nitrogen entirely with an oxygen-helium mix? This would be an excellent idea, were it not for a few other problems. As we mentioned above, helium is expensive, almost prohibitively so when it comes to blending a mix that contains over 80% helium into a scuba twin set. The £3 air fill rises to over £60. Helium, used in open circuit equipment, also induces bodily heat loss. Its thinner molecular structure may make it easier to diffuse in and out of body tissues, and have a less narcotic effect, but it also carries a considerable thermal handicap. Unlike the denser gases, which provide some degree of insulation, helium transmits heat very rapidly indeed, and in open-circuit use can remove some core body heat in exhaled gas. In cold water diving, this can increase the potential for hypothermia, decompression illness, oxygen toxicity and a number of other diving-related hazards.

Heliox, or trimix for that matter, must never be used for suit inflation – to surround the body with a molecularly-thin, heat-transmitting gas is to compound the problem of keeping warm. When mixed gases containing helium are being breathed, suit inflation is generally achieved by carrying a small cylinder (2-3 litre) of air or argon, or by using the nitrox travel mix.

Heliox mixes are non-narcotic, and can provide extended bottom times at depths of up to 30 metres. In shorter deep exposures, however, heliox can actually increase the amount of decompression required on a dive. Because helium enters the tissues so rapidly – over 2.5 times faster than nitrogen – there can be correspondingly more to diffuse out. Over the same short time period, not enough of a denser gas like nitrogen may have diffused into the tissues to require decompression. This is another reason why dilution with nitrogen to make a trimix can be advantageous – the playoff becomes one between narcosis and the decompression profile.

The nitrogen/helium decompression curves meet at around the two hour stage, and for dives lasting longer than that, there can be a considerable time advantage to be gained by using heliox. Such dives are, however, rare in recreational circles.

Though helium is non-narcotic, it can contribute to a neurological problem called High-Pressure Nervous Syndrome (HPNS) at depths in excess of 130 metres. The precise cause of this is still unknown, but is exacerbated by rapid pressurisation to depth. Again, the method of dealing with this is to introduce a little bit of nitrogen into the mix, effectively to make the diver a little more relaxed, and to make very slow descents. Using this method, dives have been made on trimixes under highly controlled conditions, with helium as the primary dilutant gas, to over 750 metres.

With the advent of mixed gas rebreathers on the technical and sport diving markets, helium-rich trimix may become the breathing gas of choice for all depths over 40 metres. Where only a couple of cubic metres are consumed on a dive lasting several hours, helium's high initial expense becomes far less significant, and its potential for reducing narcosis to tolerable levels in a trimix gives it a considerable number of advantages. For deep diving, its thinner molecular structure works to material advantage – it is easier to breathe than air, and thus flow rates of regulators and valves are less compromised by increasing gas density. There are also fewer of the long-term physiological problems found with nitrogen/oxygen diving, making helium a safer gas in physiological terms as well.

Real versus ideal gas laws

One of the not-so-obvious problems of blending trimixes is that all gases have different compressibilities. Helium does not compress as much as oxygen. A cylinder filled to 200 bar with oxygen will contain more oxygen than the same cylinder filled to 200 bar with helium. When equal quantities of the two gases are added to the same cylinder, say 100 bar of each, there will be more oxygen in the cylinder than helium.

This causes obvious problems when heliox or trimix is blended using the partial pressure method. "Ideal" gas laws allow for the simple calculation of gas components of a mixture on a percentage basis, and these percentages can easily be converted into bar equivalent. "Real" gas laws state that this is not quite so simple. In practice, an awareness of the problem is usually enough for compressing open circuit mixes – a knowledgable blender will add a little less oxygen than is called for (perhaps 10%), analyse the resulting mixture, and compensate accordingly to reach the required final pressure. The important step is the analysis of oxygen in the final mix, and that blending is carried out by a trained and competent person.

Other exotic gases

For the sake of completeness, a brief mention should be made of other inert gas mixes that have been experimented with for diving. Argon, while mentioned above as suitable for suit inflation, is certainly not suitable for breathing applications. Denser than nitrogen, it is highly narcotic at even shallower depths.

Neox (neon/oxygen) has been used, both in open-circuit and in rebreathers, but is even more expensive than helium. While non-narcotic, it is suitable only for very short dives to depth, where its greater density reduces the rate of diffusion compared with other gases, and so allows brief deep dives with no or reduced decompression. Once the diffusion threshold is passed, however, it takes ages to come out of saturation, and decompressions are unduly long.

Hydrox was used in experiments as early as 1789, with a degree of success. Unfortunately, when mixed with oxygen percentages higher than 4%, hydrogen becomes explosive. Four percent oxygen is not enough to support life until a depth of 35 metres or so is reached, so hydrox cannot be used without a gas switch at depth – and the mix switched from must not contain more than 4% oxygen! So, if air is used to descend to 35 metres, a further "flushing mix" (eg, 4% oxygen/96% nitrogen) must be used before the final switch can be made, to avoid the diver exploding.

During research in the 1980's, experimental dives by the French firm, Comex, revealed that the narcotic side effects of hydrogen below 150 metres were more dangerous than nitrogen – more akin to the effects of LSD than alcohol. So, while there may be some advantages in the use of hydrox in the mid-depth range between 35 and 150 metres, it has limited application elsewhere.

Hydreliox, a mixture of hydrogen, helium and oxygen, has been used successfully in some very deep dives. Divers from Comex have reached a depth of over 700 metres. By tailor blending a variety of inert gases with oxygen, the symptoms of HPNS, hydrogen narcosis, nitrogen narcosis and gas density may be controllable enough to allow humans to breathe mixed gases to depths of around 1000 metres (animals have already been to over 1000 metres and back). Further research is continuing into the possibility of replacing part of the blood with a fluorcarbon-based fluid that reduces gas uptake, with fluids that fill the lungs and act as gas diffusers from cryogenic breathing units or even the water itself, and with a variety of drugs that reduce the side effects of inert gas at high partial pressures. Whether the long-term future is with these, or with increasingly flexible one-atmosphere diving suits (like the Newt Suit, pictured right), only time will tell.

The Newt Suit.

Diving in an overhead environment.

CHAPTER SIX

Overhead environments

DEALING WITH unusual environments usually requires unusual skills. This is true above and below water, where a number of environments have "hard" roofs. The list that can be encountered below water is legion, ranging from wrecks, caves and ice-covered seas and lakes to pipelines, polluted waters and nuclear reactor tanks. The latter are of little interest to most divers, but wrecks, caves and ice are traditionally the realm of the technical diver. It is these we are concerned with here, and with the basic rules for surviving safely in such places.

They have a lot in common. Together with decompression diving, they form what are increasingly referred to as overhead environments, places with an effective "roof" above the diver that prevents him or her from surfacing, whether for simple physical reasons or because he or she will get bent by doing so. In all these environments, the surface is not immediately available as a safe refuge in a crisis.

All of these environments demand that the diver be self-contained in the extreme; there can be no "aim-for-the-surface" if out of air. So it follows that the diver alone must be capable of solving any life-threatening crisis. This can only be assured by good training and by carrying "redundant" equipment that ensures that the failure of any single item will not immediately negate survival. Both of these are crucial; it is no good knowing what to do if there is not the wherewithal to do it, nor is there any point in having the equipment, if you do not know how to react to the crisis in time.

More than anything else, it is essential to have proper training in the use of lines, lights and the appropriate equipment and techniques before launching yourself into an overhead environment. You will then have a much better chance of coming out of it alive.

Guidelines

Whether the diver is penetrating a wreck, swimming up the passages of an underwater cave, or plunging into the cold, clear waters below a surface of ice, he or she must be linked to his or her point of entry by a continuous guideline. This must be strong enough to support a steady pull, and thick enough to be clearly visible. If on a reel, then a thickness between 2mm and 6mm may be appropriate, getting thicker where visibility is poor, currents are strong, temperature is colder or the potential for entanglement or line abrasion is high. While line can be fed from the surface, the diver generally has more control over his or her own destiny if it is run from a reel he or she is directly controlling.

The reel itself should be properly constructed and capable of being used and controlled by one hand. Its balance should be good, and it should be

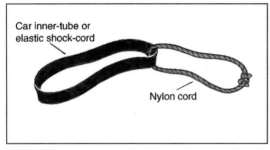

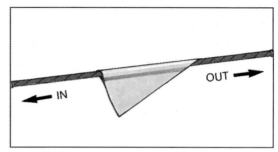

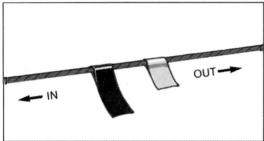

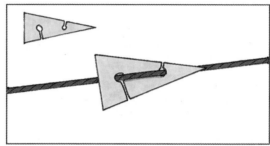

Top left: Snoopy loops. Above left: Tape line markers. Top right: Direction marker on line. Above right: Plastic line marker.

designed so that the line cannot be come tangled around the spindle. It should be able to contain the appropriate amount of line without over-flowing, which would encourage the line to spill out in the water, usually at the most inconvenient point of the dive. It should have some type of self-locking mechanism so that it can be locked firmly when not in active use. Few reels available on the SCUBA market today fulfil all these requirements.

When laying a guideline, the line should be kept reasonably taut, ideally by controlling the line reel with one hand and tensioning the line with the other. The diver should be very aware of their surroundings, and should continually be making sure that the line is in the best position for the return swim, and not dragging into low section or impenetrable parts of the wreck/ice/cave, or into deep sediment banks where visibility could be compromised on the return.

To ensure this, the line will probably have to be belayed at regular intervals. This can be as simple as putting a couple of wraps in half-hitch form round a protruding stake or spar. Where no suitable natural belays exist, lead weights, large stones or other heavy objects can be used to fasten the line to in an appropriate part of the passageway. If nothing of a suitable size is around, small net bags can be carried so that a variety of smaller objects can be gathered together in the bag to form a suitable weight, or "snoopy-loops" – a cave diving trick – can be used. These are made by cutting circles from a car inner tube and tying loops of cord through the rubber ring. The stretchy rubber circles can be stretched across suitable projections after the guideline has been looped through the cord rings.)

However inventive the method of belaying, (and there are as many ways of belaying line as there are divers to invent them) care must be taken to ensure its permanence. Snoopy loops, while quite adequate for a couple of penetrations, are not long-term options, and should be replaced if regular

Cave diver laying a line, keeping it well clear of his body.

dives are to be made at the site . Regular use will also wear the guideline, and thicker line should be laid where regular diving is envisaged.

If a complex wreck or cave is being explored, or if lines lead in several directions from a single opening in ice, make sure that they are properly marked. If they head to a particular place, mark them with the name of the place. If they belong to a particular group, mark the names of the divers in that group.

Where lines diverge underwater, keep the junctions simple. To avoid confusion, always have a clear indication of which way is out (see below). Consider, with a semi-permanent or permanent line, actually separating line junctions by at least a few centimetres, to avoid the potential for a diver who is feeling his/her way back along the main line in darkness missing the correct way for "out", whilst a diver emerging in darkness from a side tunnel can realise that they have reached the main line, and can reach across for it. Use different colour lines for main routes and side routes.

It is always worth marking the way out clearly, at regular intervals. If a diver becomes separated from the guideline (and remember most overhead environments are dark or have reduced light) he/she may take some time to find it again. Assuming they do find it, they need a rapid indication, with dwindling gas reserves, of which way is out.

Types of line reels.

At line junctions, clearly mark the outward line with a removable marker - either a clothes peg or a plastic line arrow (see below). Where more than one group is in the same area, use different coloured markers, removing only your own on exit.

Typical methods include the use of bi-coloured tags (which can also double as survey markers) every 5 metres on the line, with a yellow tag indicating "out" and a black tag indicating "in". These are made simply with electrical tape, winding it round the line, or through the lay if laid line is used. Another method is to use direction arrows, which should always point to the nearest exit. These can either be of Gaffer (or Duct) Tape folded over on itself, or a drilled piece of plastic sheet into which the line can be hooked.

All lines should be removed on exit, unless there is a good reason for leaving them in. If you leave them, you should take responsibility for their upkeep until removal. Abandoned lines eventually fray and break in currents, and present a real hazard to future explorers. Remember, however, that wet line being wound back on to a reel underwater usually takes up much more space than dry line being carefully wound on to the reel on the surface before a dive.

Jump reels

Though the diver should always be in touch-contact with a guideline, accidents do happen. If the line is lost, then it must be found again as quickly as possible, and as effectively as possible. Where visibility is bad, or the environment a complex shape, it is little use blindly swimming around and hoping to bump into it, even if direction markings are present. Diving takes place in a three dimensional environment, and the line may easily be above or below the diver, not simply off to one side.

Assuming you have not strayed too far from the point at which you lost the line, then retrieval may be easy. Cave divers have developed the habit of taking an emergency reel, or "jump-reel", containing a few metres of thin line that acts as a back up for crisis moments like this. The end of the line contains a small drop-weight,

Line reels.

and either this can be used or the line can be tied off to a local projection, and a series of circular sweep searches made in all directions until the original line is found.

In a passageway, once a wall has been located it should be followed laterally, up, across the roof, and down the other side, tracking back across the floor until the belay point is regained. The odds are that the original line will have been snared by the search line and looped back into your grasp. If you have still not found it, move in the direction you think the line lies for the distance of your search line, make a new belay, retrieve the search line, and start again. It may be worth waiting a few moments for the water to clear slightly, and looking for any traces of current, fin marks, or details that may suggest a direction. In such situations it pays to be slow and methodical in your approach. Occasional compass readings taken on the way in will help orientate you, and may provide a clue as to which way the exit lies.

Jump reels can also be used to make brief forays off the main line, or to bridge gaps between permanent lines. Anyone encountering a jump-reel underwater should remember that someone may actually be using it at the time, and should NEVER remove it. Where multiple parties may be using a single jump line to bridge a gap, then a system of coloured markers (eg, clothes pegs) placed on entry and removed on exit may be sufficient to tell diving teams when everyone is out.

Lights

If it is dark, then you must use lights. Each diver should carry at least three, because batteries run out, bulbs fail, and seals leak. Try not to run all your lights at once, but maintain at least one in reserve. Make sure each of them has enough power to run at least twice the planned duration of the dive.

Many cave divers mount two smaller torches on hard helmets, both to leave their hands uncluttered and so that, as they turn their heads, the lights follow their eyes. A larger, hand-held torch helps avoid back-scatter from particles in the water, making the best use of the available visibility. If you are not wearing a helmet then hang the spare torches from your harness in easily retrievable positions, and where they are protected from abuse from the environment. Use small loops of elastic cord or inner tube to hold them closely to the harness, helmet or arm, while still allowing rapid removal.

Lighting systems for the technical diver.

When you need to communicate with another diver, do ensure that your torches are not shining directly into the face and eyes of the other diver, but point them at your hands, or your slate, or at whatever feature you wish the diver to see. Look obliquely at anyone who is trying to communicate with you, and make sure that neither your eyes nor their eyes are blinded by an ill-directed light.

The wattage of light carried affects your ability to see less than you may believe. Accustomisation of a diver's eyes to light can make even a smallish light seem bright. Where a team of divers carries a widely different range of lights, then the divers with lower wattage bulbs, or non-halogen bulbs, may literally be left in the dark by their companions. Try, when diving as a team, to take a lighting setup that complements those of the other members of the team. It is no good having the brightest torch in the group if it destroys the accustomisation of your companion's eyes.

As a team, however, it is worth taking the best lights you can find. For truly dark cave or wreck dives, a main light with an output of between 35 and 75 watts is ideal. Good lighting reduces stress, increases environmental awareness by revealing more detail, and generally makes the dive more pleasurable. Secondary lights should be strong enough to enable you to see clearly in your immediate vicinity, and to find the way out.

In a dark environment, lighting can also become a primary means of communication. American cave divers have developed a simple series of signals which cover the immediate range of attention-grabbing questions. A circular motion with a light indicates the OK sign, and can be used to ask "Are you OK?" or to reply "Yes, I am OK". Energetic flashing of a light, by vigorous side-to-side or up-and-down sweeps, is an "Emergency" or "Attention" sign.

Both such messages must be given with definite movements, and are much easier to give with a hand-held light. They should be flashed where the other diver can see them, and ideally not directly into his/her face. It is of little use blinding a diver who is trying to help you solve a problem. Play the light off the wall the diver is looking at. If you are diving in a dark environment with a companion, do make a point of visually checking their location and condition more often.

Equipment

To dive safely below a solid surface, or on long decompressions, you must carry the appropriate equipment. What that equipment is, and how you wear it, will depend to a degree on the physical constraints of the environment. Small, constricted openings and passageways in a cave or wreck may mean it is more sensible to wear your cylinders on your sides, to protect them from damage from the roof or walls of the passage.

There are several proprietary harnesses for mounting cylinders in such a fashion, but the key thing is that they should stay in place, and not swivel round the divers hips unnecessarily. Where sediments or rough floors dictate additional streamlining, side-mounted cylinders should have additional fastenings from their necks, with some kind of additional loop, to a chest harness. This ensures that the cylinders lie straight along the diver's sides, and that the first stages of regulators do not get damaged by unnecessary physical contact with the floor.

Where back-mounted cylinders are used, it is good practice either to invert them (so that the cylinder

Side mounted cylinders.

Back mounted system.

valves can be easily reached in a constriction, and to provide a degree of protection from the roof), or to place a cage over them, to protect them from contact damage. Again, nothing should be allowed to dangle unduly from the diver, to avoid reducing visibility by dragged equipment stirring up silt banks, or to allow damage by, or to, the diver through contact with the environment.

Once more, the key word is redundancy. Take at least two of everything on which your life depends. Two lights (or more), two independent breathing systems (regulator, cylinder, contents gauge), decompression meters and depth gauges, watches or dive timers, masks and knives, buoyancy compensators and anything else which may be appropriate for the dive.

Gas management

On each and every dive, gas management is of critical importance. Getting into the water without knowing how long your gas is going to last is like heading up the motorway with an unknown amount of petrol in your tank. It may get you there, but then again...you never know if it is going to run out in the fast lane , in the middle of overtaking a very large lorry.

The rule of thirds

Stated quite simply, this gas management rule suggests that you use one-third of your air for the inward swim, one-third for swimming out, and that you keep one-third of the supply for emergencies. If two or more cylinders are used, this law applies to EACH cylinder. The first cylinder is breathed down for one third of its contents, then an exchange is made to the second cylinder, and so on. The process is repeated on the return.

If two cylinders are being used, the failure of one system should still leave the diver with enough gas in the other set to return safely to base. Though decompression stops may be made on the cylinders carried by the diver, a separate source of breathing gas should be left at the decompression stop as an additional safety factor, in case a system failure reduces the gas supply or an emergency prolongs the dive.

In high currents, or when using DPV's (see Chapter 8) it may be appropriate to alter the Third's Rule to a Fourth's or Fifth's Rule, where a return swim may have to be made against a strong current flow, or without the use of the vehicle. In such cases proper dive planning should include a look at gas consumption and emergency requirements for these specific conditions.

Calculating gas requirements

A diver resting at the surface can breathe anything between 10 and 20 litres of gas per minute at rest. Under stress or workload, this can increase to 30-60 litres per minute. To find how this equates to gas consumption at depth, we use two simple formulae, which involve knowing the depth and the gas (not the water) capacity of the diver's cylinder in litres.

These are:

T = V/(Pa x R)
and **V = Pa x R x T**

where **T** = time in minutes, **V** = volume in free litres, **Pa** = absolute pressure in bar and **R** = Ventilation volume per minute in litres.

One thousand free litres equal one cubic metre. To find out the volumetric content of a cylinder in free litres, we must use the following equation:

C = VW x WP

where **C** = contents in free litres, **VW** = cylinder volume in litres of water, and **WP** = Working Pressure in bar.

For example, to find out how many free litres af gas a 12 litre, 232 bar cylinder would contain, the formula would read:

12 x 232 = 2784 litres of free gas

If we breathe 30 litres per minute of free gas at the surface, this cylinder would last for about 93 minutes. To calculate the duration at 80 metres we use

T = V/(Pa x R)
T = 2784 / (9 x 30)
T = 10.3 minutes

Using the Rule of Thirds, this would give us a maximum bottom time of just over three minutes before starting the return trip.

Gas management is extremely important on long duration, overhead environment or on deep dives. Whereas on shorter dives it is quite possible to wear one or two cylinders and know that you have plenty of gas in reserve to cope with any reasonable eventuality, the same is never true when time and depth are both part of an irregular equation. Make a habit of using the above formulae to compute gas requirements, and get into the habit of keeping a record of just how long your cylinders last, when full, at particular depths. Remember that gas consumption increases in times of stress , and compute reserves for a breathing rate of 60 litres a minute to give yourself an indication of how quickly your planned reserves could be used up in a crisis. The 12 litre cylinder, (see table) in a crisis at 80 metres, might last just over 5 minutes. Would that be adequate in an emergency?

Additional supplies can be staged on the dive, either by carrying them with you as additional cylinders, or by placing them at points along the route

CYLINDER SIZES AND PRESSURES

Water Capacity	200 bar	232 bar	300 bar
3 litres	600	696	900
5 litres	1000	1160	1500
7 litres	1400	1624	2100
10 litres	2000	2320	3000
12 litres	2400	2784	3600
15 litres	3000	3480	4500

into the wreck or cave. Where multiple gas mixtures are being used, each stage cylinder should be clearly marked with the appropriate mix name and gas percentage contents.

Wrecks

Wrecks provide their own particular environmental hazards. Divers familiar with the problems of external structures on wrecks should realise that these are compounded when penetration of the wreck takes place. A wreck is a decaying structure. It can be likened to an abandoned mine, where the natural environment is slowly reducing the man-made elements to a point of eventual collapse and total decay.

To enter a wreck is to enter an inherently unsafe environment. Depending on the reasons for the wreck being there, and the time elapsed since its sinking, the structure may or may not be sound. Air bubbles trapped against a roof exert a positive pressure, effectively "lifting" the roof, and possibly creating stresses that cause collapse. The same bubbles can disturb silt lying on the roof and walls, or even in the rooms above, which can filter down and reduce visibility on exit, even if no silt is visible on the swim in. Once the collapse of a structure starts , it can accelerate very quickly, and a series of progressive collapses can quickly occur, trapping a diver inside. Sediments from one diver's passing can cloud the water for others, and currents in a wreck can distribute such sediments some distance from their original site of disturbance.

When laying lines inside a wreck you should take into account the stresses placed laterally on chosen belays, and you should take care to avoid any sharp or unduly rough corners where the line might be chafed through. Care should be taken not to dislodge any hatchways or doors, which may close and trap the diver. In general, the older the wreck, the more care should be taken when entering its structure. If in doubt, always leave a properly equipped diver at the point of entry to assist in an emergency.

Deeper wrecks often appear more sound, due to a lack of wave or storm influence to encourage breakup. This does not necessarily mean that they are

Sump divers preparing to pass a flooded cave.

– the biological effect of boring worms and slow material decay can leave them even more fragile, awaiting the merest nudge from bubbles, fins or tanks to collapse. Remember, problem solving at depth is more dangerous, there is a time limit, and a decompression penalty that increases with every second that passes. If in doubt, stay out!

The main dangers of cave diving

Caves

Just because you are a competent diver, and are skilled in line handling and the penetration of wrecks, this does not mean you are competent to cave dive. Caves are natural environments with their own problems; problems of structure, sedimentation, and water flow that require an understanding of how and why caves "work". Many of the problems encountered in cave diving are diving related, and can be solved with diving skills; many are not. The sense of claustrophobia, of enclosure, can be much greater in a cave than in a wreck. Whilst passages are generally sound, there are places where they are not, and it may need a trained eye to spot them. Depth and distance are very hard to measure in a cave, and it is easy to think you are not in as far, or as deep, as you actually are.

In certain parts of the world, like North Florida, cave diving tends to be carried out from the surface, the divers entering springs, or resurgences, where the water flows out of the ground. Here, diving skills are required from the word go, and caving skills may take more of a second place. But more than 20 divers a year still die in these Florida caves, mostly those who lack training or the proper equipment for penetrating such environments. As with all extreme diving environments, what seems safe is only safe until things start to go wrong.

In the UK and Europe, many cave dives start at the bottom of air-filled cave systems, and the diver must be a caver before they even reach the water, much less enter it. Even resurgences are different propositions – the water is generally peat-stained, cold and dark, visibility is low, and, being river caves, much sediment is present. Proper training with a responsible authority is essential before cave diving is undertaken.

Ice

Ice diving involves more than just overhead environment skills. It too demands a high level of equipment knowledge, and an understanding of what this particular environment requires of that equipment. Regulators must have adequate protection to stop their first stages free-flowing, and many of those which offer a "silicone cap" for cold-water diving do not really stand up to ice diving.

The best way to get information on an extreme diving environment is to ask someone who dives in it regularly. As equipment changes, those who regularly use it in particular environments stay abreast of developments and will be able to advise what is the most appropriate equipment in current production.

There are two different types of environment where serious under ice div-

Special accessories are needed for cold-water diving.

ing may take place – low altitude/high latitude and high altitude. Each has subtle differences in approach.

The former, low altitude/high latitude, assumes that you are diving under marine or freshwater ice where the surface climate is also extremely cold . Your choice of thermal clothing should reflect this, allowing minimal penetration of water to the skin while immersed, and the potential for a rapid change of clothes in sheltered conditions on the surface. Divers undertaking this sort of diving must be physically fit, more so than in most other aquatic environments, due to the harsh environmental conditions posed by the water itself.

Holes in the ice should be surrounded by warm, windproof staging areas, and should ideally be triangular in shape, allowing the diver to pull themself easily from the water with their elbows, and providing space for the cylinders to emerge behind their back. The diving tender who stays in the shelter should be as well equipped as the diver when it comes to withstanding cold. He is there to assist the diver in and out of the hole, and a hypothermic assistant with frostbitten hands is a liability rather than an asset.

The diver can be dressed in whatever type of drysuit he feels comfortable in, but should bear in mind the thermal qualities of that suit at the working depth. Foam neoprene is fine at shallow working depths, but hypothermic at greater depths if not used with suitable undergarments. A compressed neoprene or membrane suit needs a layered system of undergarments (silk or polypropylene next to the skin, with pile, pelt, or 400g grade Thinsulate™). Drysuit gloves or mittens which seal directly on to the suit cuffs are ideal – dry hands greatly improve manual dexterity and stay warm longer. Full-face masks (see Chapter 8) provide a better degree of thermal protection than a half-mask, but cold water hoods with neoprene protectors for chin, lips and forehead may also be used. Half-masks should cover as much of the diver's face as possible.

Regulators continually cause problems with freeze-up and free flow. This problem can be reduced by not breathing through the regulator till submerged, and then breathing in a slow, even manner. If the air breathed is kept very dry, this will also help avoid regulator freezing. Fluid intake should be increased to allow for the additional degree of dehydration caused by very dry air. Older, single-stage twin hose regulators are still popular in ice diving, experience having proved themselves very reliable at shallow depth, and less prone to freezing. One of these can be used as a main regulator, with a double stage regulator on the diver's second cylinder acting as a reserve. Use of a manifold will allow the double-hose regulator access to the air in both cylinders.

Rebreathers can be used in very cold water, but the CO_2 absorbent and batteries do not last as long as in temperate and tropical waters.

Line laying and management under ice is an art in itself, with manual dexterity often limited by thick mittens. In the absence of natural belays, empty plastic containers can be filled with air to keep the line resting against the roof, and these can be jammed into hollows or fissures in the ice to stop them drifting. A flashing light or a chemical light in the entrance can help orientation.

Although free-flow situations and dry-suit blow-ups commonly occur, the number one cause of fatality in ice diving remains getting lost. Anything that can be done by the team to reduce that possibility is a high priority.

High altitude diving requires additional skills. By high altitude, I mean over 3000 metres, where the atmospheric pressure is considerably less than at sea level. High altitude usually equates directly with remoteness, and all the problems of diving in remote locations compound the dangers. Divers should make sure they are sufficiently acclimatised to the altitude before commencing a diving programme, spending at least 24 hours at the site before diving. Sleeping at a slightly lower altitude offers an additional safety factor.

All equipment that contain seals that operate across a pressure gradient (eg, underwater cameras, torches, some depth gauges) should be disassembled and adjusted to the working altitude (and back again, on descent). Wetsuits of closed cell neoprene may expand, and become stiff and unwieldy, so dry membrane or compressed neoprene suits with appropriate undergarments are perhaps better.

Many decompression tables allow altitude adjustments to be made, and tables where adjustments are tried and tested are preferred. No really tried tables exist for altitudes above 3000 metres, but Tom Hennessy (1977) recommended the following formula be used to convert actual depth to table depth:

$$\textbf{Depth (tables)} = \frac{\textbf{2 x actual depth}}{\textbf{(Barometric pressure + 1)}}$$

(Note that barometric pressure must be expressed in bars)

Oxygen has been used for decompression at high altitude, but any gas mixtures are experimental at high altitudes . Try to avoid decompression diving wherever possible. Nitrox has some advantage at altitude, and a mixture can be made that tailors the partial pressure of oxygen and nitrogen to equal that of sea-level air at the target depth, allowing standard tables to be used.

For diving in pipelines, polluted waters and nuclear reactor tanks, you must seek elsewhere for information. These do not come within the scope of this volume, though you might refer to the *UNESCO Code of Practice for Scientific Diving*, where these and many other unusual environments that may be of interest to the more specialised members of the diving fraternity are examined in detail.

CHAPTER SEVEN

Emergencies

BEARING IN MIND that technical diving is a more extreme form of a recreational activity, and is more advanced than many professional applications of diving, the potential for accident may well be higher. A technical diver should be better versed in the response to incidents both in and out of the water, and a degree of first aid training with a diving bias is strongly advised. This chapter looks at some of the incidents that may arise in sport and technical diving, and the appropriate responses to them. Remember that, in every case, your own safety is paramount. Do not unnecessarily endanger your own life going to the aid of someone whose survival is already doubtful.

Physical problems

These can be divided into two main parts — bodily damage to the diver and the effect of the physical environment around the diver. The former can be due to an enormous variety of causes, the latter largely relates to the diver no longer being in control of his or her surroundings.

Physical trauma

Physical trauma is the result of actual bodily damage, either through embolism (see below) or tissue damage of some description — a cut, bite, blow or break. The best way to deal with such damage is to be properly medically trained in first aid. Otherwise, do what you can. Get the casualty out of the water and somewhere safe, stop any bleeding quickly and as best you can — ideally by use of a pressure pad or bandage and elevating the wound, but use a tourniquet in extreme cases if bleeding is excessive at first . Do release it gently every few minutes, to allow some blood flow to the affected limb until the bleeding has stopped enough to be controlled by a pressure pad.

If bones are broken, simply try to immobilise the limb, and do not move it unnecessarily. Unless you know exactly what to do, it is sometimes best to try not to make things worse.

Once the initial response has been made (or during it, if feasible), make sure help is summoned as quickly as possible, and get the casualty to a hospital, by the fastest means available. In transit, keep them warm and well-wrapped. If internal injuries are suspected, do not give them any drinks or food; if there are no internal injuries, a hot drink is a good idea if the casualty is conscious. Leave someone with them to reassure them at all times, and try to ensure that they lie down rather than sit. If they are in shock, and no-one else is in danger of DCI, use some therapeutic oxygen on them.

If in doubt, be pessimistic. It is sometimes better to over-treat rather than under-treat, and never assume someone is OK merely because they say they are.

Stings and bites

Bites usually require treatment as for trauma above, but some smaller ones may, like the majority of stings, be venomous, and require alternative treatment on site. Whilst the best way of avoiding stings or bites is to avoid touching anything unnecessarily, and to wear gloves, such advice is of little use after the event. Where there is a possibility that lengthy decompression will be required before surfacing, the need for care is even greater. You may be faced with the choice of dying from a toxic wound, or betting bent!

Toxic stings and bites can be broken down into two main groups.

1 Stings from coral, hydroids and most jellyfish (except the sea wasp)
The main problem with technical diving may be due to being stung during a long decompression. Though there is little that can be done in the water, you can at least make sure things do not get worse. If stinging creatures are present in the plankton, make sure you are adequately covered to start with, and that you are offering as little skin as possible to be stung on. If stung, keep things from getting worse and, unless the pain is unbearable, finish the decompression if possible. In a case of severe stinging from a jellyfish, avoid rubbing the area and try and avoid contact between the affected skin and other parts of the body. The unused toxic cells are still active, and can strike afresh. If stung by something REALLY toxic, get out of the water and aim for medical treatment ashore, in a recompression chamber if necessary.

Once out of the water, vinegar, citrus or acetic acid will ease the irritation caused by minor injuries. Use ammonia solution if available. Weals raised by jellyfish stings should not be allowed to get infected further, and it is best to cover these properly, or refrain from diving until the wound is sufficiently healed. Very gently clean the area with wet sand and rinse the skin with dilute ammonia or a solution of baking soda. Meat tenderiser, especially if it contains papain, an extract of papaya, can also help relieve pain. Once the skin and surrounding area is thoroughly clean, apply antihistamine ointment or cortisone cream, and treat any secondary symptoms that may be present, such as shock. Seek medical advice from a specialist physician if necessary.

2 Puncture wounds from venomous fish
Symptoms vary. Sometimes there is intense pain, local swelling and a general feeling of malaise. Breathing may be affected, and in some cases the wound may be fatal. Victims should surface and seek proper medical attention as quickly as possible. Again, decompression should be omitted where necessary – it is now a question of priorities.

Victims should be treated for shock, the wound opened and cleaned of all foreign matter (bits of fish spine, etc.) and then immersed in hot water – as hot as the victim can tolerate – for at least half-an-hour. Most such toxins are protein-based, and heat breaks down the compounds, inhibiting spreading and reducing pain. Apply a broad pressure bandage around as much of the limb as possible, with a splint to restrict movement. Do not remove the bandage and the splint until you reach a doctor who has the relevant anti-venom available.

Line or net entanglement

Where a diver becomes entangled in a fishing net, or in abandoned line, the last thing he should do is immediately struggle to get free. On a deep technical dive, where gas supplies are limited, such a problem is obviously more severe, and there is less time to resolve it, but that time must be well-spent. Take a moment or two to orientate yourself, and see which way the main bulk of the net lies. Use your light or other signal to attract your companion. Carefully start to cut yourself free – do not try to undo knots, it can take too long. Make your movements precise, and if you cannot reach, let your companion do it for you. Keep the net taut without pulling it unnecessarily – a suddenly free-floating net is a far greater problem. As soon as you are free, swim carefully some distance away before turning to check equipment and orientation. For net cutting, plaster scissors are better than knives, as they push the net away from the diver during the act of cutting.

With guidelines, make sure everyone else in the team is on the "out" side of the line before trying to do anything drastic. Try to obtain whatever slack is available, and see if you can simply unhook yourself, with the aid of a companion if available. If you are still caught, and no help is available, take a firm hold of the "out" end and reach behind to cut yourself free. Once free, if you have sufficient reserves of gas, take a moment or two to relax and then retie the line if you consider it necessary and possible. If you do not have sufficient reserves, leave it for another time, but make sure anyone else using the line knows it has been cut, otherwise it becomes your responsibility to reconnect it if it is in regular use.

Out of gas

Though an out-of-gas situation should never arise if gas supplies are monitored and gas reserves planned, it occasionally does.

This is one of the situations when diving with a companion can make all the difference. A properly trained team should be able to regard an out-of-gas situation as an inconvenience rather than a desperate, life-threatening hazard, and should be equipped to cope with it. Each diver should carry a 2-metre hose on one of their second stages, which allows the out-of-gas diver to comfortably swim beside his companion as they return to the surface. If both divers have been using the "Rule of Thirds", they have enough gas to return to the surface without compromising their decompression profile or their safety.

This is, however, traditionally one of the riskiest operations in diving, and several fatalities occur each year due to gas-sharing incidents, particularly where equipment is inadequate and the divers poorly trained in such skills. With untrained or ill-equipped divers, stress levels can become too high to control, gas reserves may be inadequate, and the survival instinct may lead to actual fights over equipment underwater.

The proper response is to make sure that you are adequately trained and equipped, and that you always have sufficient reserves to get you and your companion back to the surface. Too few people take sufficient gas with them for this, and rarely think through the consequences of their actions. If you wish to dive longer, or deeper, consider your companions. Make sure you have sufficient gas, and a high enough degree of redundancy in the first place to make an out-of-gas situation highly unlikely to happen.

The classic out-of-gas situation occurs when a diver has been breathing from a single cylinder through a single regulator. Either a part of the system fails to operate, or they do not monitor their consumption sufficiently well to be aware of the problem. Some run out of gas during the ascent, or the decompression, because they do not know their own gas consumption rates (see Chapter 6).

Do take time to plan your gas supply properly on a technical dive – beware of taking what "looks like enough". It's also worth practising swimming with full equipment in a swimming pool or sheltered water just to practice gas sharing in full technical gear, and to see how far you can swim to a companion when out of gas, having just exhaled. The best way to deal with any emergency is to have practised the response first.

Agree beforehand which regulator is the one to go for first in an emergency. There is no right or wrong answer here, some people prefer the victim to go for the one in their mouth, some prefer an immediate move for the reserve. In the latter case, make sure you both know exactly where that will be on each diver during the dive. If your companion comes towards you making an out-of-gas signal, get the reserve regulator ready for him. Make the whole process as stress-free as possible. Equally, if you are running low on gas, do not leave it to the last moment to inform your companion.

Lost diver

It is always possible to lose one of your team. Someone may get swept from a wreck in strong currents, disoriented and lose the way back to the anchor line, be forced into a free-hang decompression, or be a victim of one of a number of other possible scenarios.

If you see someone lose contact and get swept away, take a compass bearing on the direction in which they went, gather the rest of the group and surface as quickly as you can. Let the surface boat float down current, if the surface current is flowing in the same direction as on the bottom. Keep a lookout on all sides for the lost diver, who may have been taken some distance from the boat by the time you surfaced, and who may be decompressing below an emergency buoy. As surface currents and bottom currents do not always flow in the same direction, do not expect to see the diver ahead of the boat. Your compass bearing on the bottom may give you some clue, but do not rely on it.

Inform the emergency services immediately, and give them your precise location, now and the time at which the victim went missing. Once they are in the area, the primary responsibility becomes theirs, and you may be better returning to base to provide what further help you can from there.

If you are the diver who gets lost, do not panic. If it is impossible to make your way back to a safe point, analyse your situation. Get your buoyancy under control, and make your way towards the surface as quickly and as carefully as possible. If you have a decompression reel and float, release them as soon as your decompression line will reach the surface. It will provide a marker that others may see, even before you start decompressing. Complete your decompression, and leave your buoy inflated to act as an emergency marker. Stay with it, and do not attempt to swim for shore, unless the shore is close by and there are no inopportune currents. Remember, the buoy is easier to spot than you are.

If a diver is lost inside a wreck, or other overhead environment (OHE), the options become more limited. Only the most experienced divers should penetrate the OHE to look for him, and they must be attached to a line, or take one with them. A lost diver may well be a panicking diver, and possibly low on gas, and so the rescue diver should have a spare gas source ready for immediate assistance. The rescue diver should take due account of their own position, and not endanger their own lives unduly by continuing a search beyond the limits of their safe gas reserves or their distance lines. One person dying is quite enough. If it becomes obvious that the victim will no longer be alive, the search should be abandoned, and the authorities informed so that the appropriate recovery activities can take place.

Again, the best way to ensure such searches are unnecessary is to make sure they are not required in the first place. Due attention to dive plans, redundant equipment, proper line use and the sense to change dive plans if conditions are inappropriate should reduce the need for emergency action to almost zero.

Gas toxicity

Oxygen toxicity

Though mentioned before, this has a place here amongst the crises. If you personally feel the onset of toxicity symptoms, do not wait to see what happens next. Ascend immediately in a controlled manner, signalling to your companion/s as you do. The onset of convulsions may be imminent! The symptoms will be alleviated by a decrease in depth, but your tissues are saturated and convulsions may occur at any time, whatever your depth. Do not let your ascent get out of control; if you do start to convulse during an uncontrolled ascent, you will almost certainly embolise before you reach the surface.

If a companion convulses in the water with you, then unless you can get behind them safely and keep their regulator in their mouth, wait till the convulsions cease. Once the diver goes limp, get them to the surface as quickly as possible. Omit any required decompression, as the diver will almost certainly have drowned unless the regulator has been retained. It is better to treat for decompression illness than for death. Make sure any gas in the lungs is evacuated properly during ascent, to avoid embolism. Once out of the water, summon assistance immediately, and if decompression has been omitted, get both of you to a recompression chamber as soon as possible . Treat the casualty as appropriate for drowning or shock while this help is being summoned. If there is omitted decompression, put both divers on oxygen. Do not omit to give the victim pure O_2 because he/she has recently convulsed – your priority is now to get nitrogen out of the system.

If the diver recovers during the ascent, and is fully conscious and breathing normally, then any required decompression stops may be made. Observe the victim closely at all times during the decompression, and ensure that they seek medical treatment as soon as they are out of the water. Do not let them dive again before a medical check-up, and DO NOT, whatever you do, let them continue the dive!

To avoid oxygen toxicity, stay within the observed safety limits. Do not, at any time, exceed a partial pressure of 1.6 bar of oxygen while in the water, and maintain appropriate time limoits for the partial pressures you are breathing. Avoid mixing high PPO2s and high work rates, overheating or CO_2 retention, and never use decongestants such as Sudafed when diving. Amongst the side effects of Sudafed and Actifed, when taken in large doses, are convulsions and respiratory difficulty, and both act as a stimulant to the central nervous system. They may act as a stimulant to the onset of oxygen toxicity, and their use has been banned by several major commercial diving companies.

Nitrogen narcosis

Nitrogen narcosis is still one of the primary problems on deep technical dives. Even using trimix, the nitrogen content of the gas can be enough to introduce a dangerous level of narcosis at depth. The only treatment for narcosis is to decrease depth, at which point the effects will reduce and disappear quite quickly. Do stay in the habit of observing companions for signs of narcosis, even on trimix dives. One of the usual effects of narcosis on an experienced diver is an enhancement of the refusal to admit to it. Do not push it; go back, mix a different trimix, and try again.

Decompression related incidents

Omitted decompression

If a diver surfaces having omitted decompression for whatever reason, they have two options open to them. Depending on how much decompression has been omitted, and the distance they are in time from a recompression chamber, they can choose to stay on the surface, ideally breathing pure O_2, and head for a chamber as soon as possible, or they can re-enter the water and complete an appropriate decompression schedule.

Though the latter is not really recommended, it is sometimes the only way to avoid DCI if a chamber is several hours distant and/or adequate oxygen is not available at the surface. It should not be confused with in-water treatment of DCI, which is an entirely different matter (see below).

Re-entry should be virtually immediate, and certainly within 3-5 minutes of reaching the surface. It is not enough to follow the omitted schedule. The standard US Navy procedure for many years was as follows:

- Repeat all stops below 12 metres
- Stay at 12 metres for $1/4$ of the 3 metre stop time plus any remaining time scheduled at 12 metres.
- At 9 metres, stay for $1/3$ of the 3 metre stop time plus any time that may be remaining at 9 metres.
- At 6 metres, spend half the 3 metre stop time.
- Stay at 3 metres for one and a half times the scheduled 3 metre stop time.
- Take 1 minute to ascend between stops.

If nitrox is available, use it throughout the decompression, making sure the PPO_2 does not exceed 1.6 bar. If pure oxygen is available, use it at 6 metres, taking an air break every 25 minutes for 5 minutes. On surfacing, continue to breathe oxygen for 30 minutes. Do not dive for 24 hours. Take lots of fluids to rehydrate, and avoid exercise.

Decompression illness

Decompression illness is the result of gas bubbles forming during depressurisation from a dive. The gas bubbles that cause the problem of decompression illness (DCI) in diving are those from the inert gas component of the breathing mix. Whilst it is technically possible to get an oxygen bend, the rate of ascent necessary to induce an O_2 DCI hit would certainly massively embolise a diver, even with very O_2 rich mixtures.

Recognition of acute decompression illness

Decompression illness is often divided into two main types, Type 1 and Type 2. Type 1, commonly referred to as "pain only" is typified by pain near or at a joint, undue fatigue, a lack of mental awareness or irritable behaviour, and occasionally accompanied by a mild rash or itching feeling in areas of the skin. Type 2, generally more severe, is usually associated with damage to ,or severe effects on, the central nervous system. Symptoms can include pain, dizziness, paralysis, unconsciousness, headache or shortness of breath. A full list of symptoms for Type 1 and Type 2 DCI is given in the following table. Severe cases of DCI may be accompanied by gas embolism (see below). Initial treatment is the same for both.

Divers do occasionally get bent, even within the tables. There is no stigma attached to getting bent, and if you suspect you are, take action immediately. Too many divers deny the possibility of DCI, and refuse to accept it can happen to them. This is tantamount to pretending you have not been hit by a bus when you clearly have. Even if the symptoms do disappear by themselves (and they may not) they may also be indicative of further damage that is not readily apparent, and therapeutic treatment and medical advice should be sought. Symptoms may also be progressive, especially with Type 2 DCI, and the sooner preventative action can be taken the better!

SYMPTOMS OF ACUTE DECOMPRESSION ILLNESS

Type 1 (Pain only)
- Skin bends – blotches, skin rash, prickling of skin.
- Fatigue
- Pain in long bone joint (usually elbow, shoulder, knee)

Type 2 (CNS)
- CNS cerebral and spinal abnormalities
- Fatigue
- Dizziness (staggers), vertigo
- Paralysis or numbness, localised loss of feeling
- Headache
- Irrational behaviour – indifference, mood swings, irritability
- Lack of awareness of surroundings
- Shortness of breath
- Inability to pass urine
- Unconsciousness, collapse, syncope
- Visual disturbance, double vision, lack of focus
- Audial disturbance, local deafness
- Abdominal or lower back pain (associated with spinal symptoms)
- Convulsions

Confirmation of DCI

If DCI is suspected but not certain, it is worth taking a few minutes to confirm the diagnosis. The following examination, recommended by the Diver's Alert Network in the USA, should be performed step-by-step as set out below. Do not omit any of them!

1 Orientation:
- Does the diver know his/her name and age?
- Does the diver know their present location?
- Does the diver know the time of day, day, date, month and year?

These questions may reveal a degree of confusion, even if the diver appears alert.

2 Eyes:
- Have the diver count the number of fingers you display, using two or three different numbers. Check each eye separately and then together. Have the diver identify a distant object (check the diver's normal state of vision first).
- Tell the diver to hold his/her head still. Place your other hand directly in front of the face, about 50cm from the nose. Ask the diver to follow your hand with his/her eyes. Move your hand up and down, then from side to side. The eyes should follow your hand smoothly, not jerk to one side and return.
- Check that the pupils are equal in size

3 Face:
- Ask the diver to whistle. Look to see that both sides of the face have the same expression while whistling. Get the diver to grit his/her teeth. Feel the jaw muscles to see that they are contracted equally.
- Instruct the diver to close his/her eyes while you lightly touch your fingertips across their forehead and face to be sure sensation is present and the same everywhere. Make the diver inform you where and how you are touching them.

4 Hearing:
- Hold your hand about 75 cm from the diver's ear and rub your thumb and finger together. Can the diver hear this? Check both ears, moving your hand closer until the diver can hear it. Check several times, and confirm with your own hearing. Make sure background noise is minimal during this test, and confirm with the diver his/her normal state of hearing.

5 Swallowing reflex:
- Instruct the diver to swallow while you watch the "Adam's apple" to be sure that it moves up and down.

6 Tongue :
- Get the diver to stick out his/her tongue. It should come out of the centre of the mouth, and not deviate to either side.

7 Muscle strength:
- Get the diver to shrug his/her shoulders while you bear down on them to check for equal muscle strength.
- Check the diver's arms by bringing the diver's elbows up level with his/her shoulders, hands level with the arms, and touching the chest. Make the diver resist while you pull the arms away, push them back, and up and down. The strength should be approximately equal in both arms in all directions. Check leg strength by getting the diver to lie flat and raise and lower the legs while you gently resist the movement.

8 Sensory perception:
- Check both sides by touching as done on the face. Start at the top of the body and compare sides while moving down to cover the entire body. Use a sharp and a blunt instrument to compare perception of different stimuli (eg, a pencil tip and a cotton-bud tip). Make sure the diver confirms sensation before you change areas.

9 Balance and Co-ordination:
- Be prepared to protect the diver from additional injury while performing this test. Get the diver to stand with feet together, eyes closed and arms outstretched. The diver should be able to maintain balance if the platform is stable. Be prepared to catch a diver who falls.
- Check co-ordination by having the diver move an index finger quickly back and forwards between his/her nose and your own finger held about 50cm from the diver's face. With the diver lying down, get him/her to slide the heel of one foot down the shin of the opposite leg.
- Check these tests on both sides of the body, and watch for unusual clumsiness on either side.

The tests should be frequently repeated while awaiting transport to therapy. Any change should be recorded. If any of the tests are not normal, damage to the central nervous system should be suspected. If the diver's condition does not allow one or more of the tests above to be performed, record which tests were missed, and the reason why. The times and results of all tests performed should be written down.

Avoidance of DCI

The potential for DCI in not limited to fast ascents or omitted stops. There are many factors which may predispose a diver to DCI, and many of these are avoidable. Dehydration, hangovers, smoking, lack of physical fitness, undue body fat, tiredness, drug abuse (caffeine and nicotine are drugs, too) all contribute towards a diver's susceptibility to DCI. In the water, make sure excessive exercise is avoided at depth or during decompression, maintain the proper ascent rate, avoid provocative profiles (eg, multiple ascents or zig-zag profiles) and keep a good thermal balance. Too hot or too cold both affect the body's ability to transport dissolved gas efficiently from tissues saturation to atmosphere. If over 40, use a more conservative set of tables, and use nitrox for decompression wherever possible. Avoid alcohol for 12 hours before a dive, and avoid excessive alcohol consumption at all times. Do not drink alcohol for four hours after a decompression dive.

Right: Always hydrate before a long or deep dive.

Do take lots of isotonic fluids (eg, water, Gatorade, apple juice – avoid coffee, tea, orange juice). Treat the first hour on the surface as a decompression stop, and avoid excessive exercise, hot showers, saunas or hot tubs. The more extreme a decompression exposure, the more important it is to follow these practices, and to delay provocative exposures to temperature, alcohol and other potential DCI triggers.

When you are at a decompression stop, stay there. Do not swim around taking photographs, or otherwise straying above or below your stop. Take some light exercise to stay warm and maintain circulation, but not so much that you get out of breath, or encourage too much blood flow. Make sure when you finish your decompression that someone is there to help you out of the water. Generally the most dangerous point is as you leave the water, when the pressure gradient is highest. A high degree of effort involved in getting you and several tens of kilos of equipment out of the water may easily trigger a DCI hit. Take your gear off in the water and clip it to a shotline, or pass it to someone who can lift it out for you.

Treatment of DCI on air or nitrox

With any diver suffering from DCI, the primary treatment, whatever gas they have been breathing, is recompression as quickly as possible. For air or nitrox, standard therapy tables are entirely suitable. In the event of a diver suffering decompression illness following a nitrox dive, the primary concern must be to get him or her to the closest recompression chamber for treatment. If the diver has been breathing nitrox during the course of the dive on which the problem arose then the chances are that their injuries will be comparatively less serious than if they had been diving on air.

The amount of oxygen breathed during the course of the dive HAS NO EFFECT on the ability of the chamber to which the diver has been transferred to treat the casualty. Confusion in the diving press and amongst some less experienced chamber operators has arisen due to remarks in the diving press about treatment for mixed gas DCI being different to that for air diving. The treatment for tri-mix and heliox may prove more complex in certain cases, but nitrox should not be regarded as a mixed gas in this instance. The standard practice is to transfer the casualty to the chamber while breathing pure oxygen, and treat as for an air decompression.

Whilst there may be an accumulation of oxygen dosage in the body tissues, this should be placed in perspective. An extreme day of diving exposure, say of 3 hours breathing nitrox with a partial pressure of 1.4 bar throughout the dive (and not just at the deepest point of the dive), gives a cumulative oxygen toxicity dose of 360 units. The maximum daily dose for a single "stand-alone" day's diving is 850 units (NOAA recommended figures). The dose gained from a standard USN Table 5 oxygen therapy treatment is 333 units, and a USN Table 6 is 645 units. The maximum acceptable dose (the point at which 50% of people exhibit a 10% loss in vital capacity) is 1495 units per day. This is composed of the maximum daily OTU (Oxygen Toxicity Unit) exposure limits plus the dose gained from normal recompression therapy. Should the therapy exceed a single treatment, the oxygen dose the

AVOID DCI

- **Before the dive:**
  Hydrate
  Avoid coffee, tea, fruit juice (except apple), alcohol
  Do not smoke
  Stay warm

- **During the dive:**
  Do not overwork
  Stay warm
  Avoid zig-zag profiles
  Ascend slowly
  Maintain decompression stops

- **After the dive:**
  Keep effort to a minimum
  Hydrate
  Do not take hot showers or saunas for 2 hours
  Avoid alcohol for 4 hours

A recompression chamber control panel.

diver originally had becomes inconsequential to the dose gained by treatment.

In multi-day diving, the allowable daily dose for a continuous seven day period of diving is 350 units per day, which takes into account the cumulative effect of oxygen, and maintains the diver within exposure limits that take into account recompression therapy. As in air diving, a break of a day every few days is recommended to reduce the gas loading on body tissues. This loading comes from oxygen and nitrogen.

There is just as much potential for oxygen accumulation in the tissues on the way to the chamber. One OTU is the equivalent of breathing pure oxygen at the surface for one minute. Following a bend, a two hour trip to a chamber breathing pure oxygen entails an exposure of 120 units or so all by itself.

It should be borne in mind that oxygen toxicity in itself is not fatal. On the surface, or under therapeutic treatment, any convulsions experienced during extreme toxicity reactions are experienced under medical supervision in a nitrox atmosphere. **The patient is in NO danger of drowning after the dive or in a recompression chamber.** The casualty will be taken off nitrox/oxygen while the convulsions are taking place, then put back on it when they stop, though airway management and aspiration can occasionally pose a problem.

Finally, when considering nitrox and DCI, the following points should be borne in mind:

1 Due to reduced levels of nitrogen in the breathing mixture, the potential for DCI is reduced when compared with air.

2 Where DCI occurs due to omitted decompression, for whatever reason, the damage to tissues from the occurrence of DCI may be less than had the damage occurred following an air dive, due to enrichment by oxygen of the breathing mixture.

3 A toxic reaction to oxygen in a breathing mixture is extremely unlikely if the diver maintains his/her partial pressure of oxygen to less than 1.6 bar, and stays within time/depth limits for the mixture being breathed. This is as true for air as it is for nitrox.

4 Any adverse reaction to the cumulative effects of oxygen during a long recompression therapy will be primarily due to the oxygen dose gained from that therapy, and not from that gained during the dive. The reaction will take place under medical supervision, and is extremely unlikely to endanger the patient's life.

5. With proper training, and proper precautions, a diver is less likely to suffer DCI during the course of a recreational dive when breathing nitrox than when breathing air.

IT IS EXTREMELY DANGEROUS – AND UNJUSTIFIABLE – TO REFUSE OR REDUCE TREATMENT OF A CASUALTY SUFFERING FROM DECOMPRESSION ILLNESS FOLLOWING EITHER AN EXTREME AIR EXPOSURE OR AN ENRICHED AIR DIVE

For gas mixtures other than air or nitrox, (ie, trimix, heliox), the best information available suggests that, unless appropriate mixed gas recompression facilities are available, the diver is recompressed as for air. The oxygen loading will be no greater than that for an air or nitrox dive, as the same initial oxygen toxicity limits apply. In this case, recompression therapy takes the place of first aid. In most technical diving cases, symptoms will probably have been resolved at therapy depth.

Whilst it is always best for a diver to be breathing the gas on which he was diving during the recompression, this may not always be possible. Where rebreathers are being used for trimix or heliox dives, however, the victim may be placed in the chamber with a rebreather containing the appropriate gas mixtures, and where possible, programmed for a therapeutic partial pressure of oxygen say 1.8 – 2.0 bar). Spare CO_2 absorbent and gas canisters should be kept available, and the patient placed on an appropriate gas mix while recharge of the unit is taking place.

Whatever the mixture breathed, treatment by recompression, on air if necessary, is the primary response. Casualties not responding to air or nitrox recompression can always be transferred under pressure to a facility that can handle complex mixed gas decompressions in incidents where the exposure has been particularly deep or long. Refusal of therapeutic treatment by any medical chamber is a violation of the basic medical code, the Hippocratic Oath.

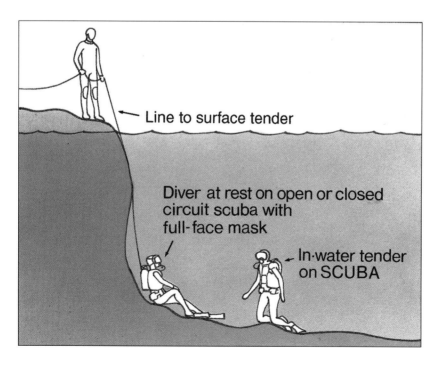

In-water recompression.

AUSTRALIAN OXYGEN IN-WATER TREATMENT TABLES

Depth (metres)	Elapsed Time in minutes	
	Mild symptoms	Serious symptoms
9	30-60	60-90
8	42-72	72-102
7	54-84	84-114
6	66-96	96-126
5	78-108	108-138
4	90-120	120-150
3	102-132	132-162
2	114-144	144-174
1	126-156	156-186

Ascent rate is 12 minutes per metre.

Note that the therapy will take from two to three hours, depending on severity of symptoms. The casualty should remain attached to the shot-line in case of convulsions. Ascent is commenced after 30 minutes if symptoms are resolved, or later (up to 90 minutes) if improvement takes longer. If symptoms recur, remain at depth a further 30 minutes before continuing the ascent. If the oxygen supply is exhausted, return to the surface rather than breathe air. After surfacing, keep the casualty at rest on a one hour on / one hour off cycle of pure oxygen and air for 24 hours, and keep fluid intake high.

In-water recompression

This is an extremely emotive issue amongst hyperbaric medics. Whilst there is no doubt that it should be avoided at all costs wherever possible, due to the inability to treat secondary injuries and the danger of O_2 toxicity, there are occasions where it is, in practice, the only option possible. In extremely remote places, in-water therapy may mean the difference between life and death, or normal life and crippling injuries.

Each situation has to be weighed very carefully. If the diver is far from a treatment base, and is exhibiting no further signs of injury other than non-complex DCI symptoms, then in-water recompression under direct supervision may be appropriate.

This is an extremely serious action that is taken when no other form of resolution is readily available. The diver and the tender/s must be prepared to spend several hours in the water, and there must be suitable equipment and gas supplies available to ensure a safe therapeutic treatment. The casualty should be fitted with a full-face mask, and dressed in warm underclothing and a drysuit, or a warm and well-fitting wetsuit in tropical waters. In-water recompression in cold water will probably expose the diver to levels of hypothermia that may prove fatal. This is probably not a cold water option.

Air should not be used as a therapy gas. Additional nitrogen loading may well compound the problem. In an ideal case, surface-supplied oxygen should be fed by umbilical to the diver, via a full-face mask. The Australians developed a method for in-water recompression that is given below. The diver MUST be accompanied by an supervising attendant at all times, and the attendant should be replaced at regular intervals to avoid compromising his/her decompression and exposure levels. Some form of communication should exist between the casualty, the supervisor and the surface. A tagged shotline should be laid to indicate precise depths, and some sort of harness should be provided to reduce physical strain on the casualty where a hard surface is not available on which to lie.

In-water recompression using a rebreather

If rebreathers are available, the following emergency procedure may be suitable. It should be emphasised that this is just as drastic as the above treatment, and should not be done if a chamber is within reach. This procedure was developed by the US Navy for use with oxygen rebreathers.

1. Put the casualty on the rebreather, ideally with a full-face mask and communications, and purge the unit at least three times with pure O_2. Disable the inert gas supply by either switching the supply off or replacing it with an O_2 cylinder.

2. Descend to a depth of 9 metres with a supervising attendant.
3. Remain there for 60 minutes for Type 1 symptoms or 90 minutes for Type 2. Ascend to 6 metres after 90 minutes whether symptoms are resolved or not.
4. Decompress to the surface by taking 60 minute stops at 6 metres and 3 metres.
5. After surfacing, continue to breathe pure O₂ for three hours.

In both cases, make sure the casualty is in continual contact with the attendant and the surface, and receives a regular supply of liquids to drink (in, for example, flexible containers with straws, or babies' bottles).

Again, remember that this is an absolute last resort. If a chamber is within five hours travel time, it is far better to place the casualty at rest, on oxygen, with plenty of appropriate fluids to drink, and transport him/her to the chamber as quickly as possible. If you must dive in remote locations consider taking a portable recompression chamber whenever possible (see Chapter 8).

Gas embolism and pulmonary barotrauma

Gas embolism, like decompression illness, is caused by over-rapid depressurisation from depth. Unlike DCI, the resulting symptoms may be physically traumatic, involving, in the worst of cases, an actual burst lung or associated pneumothoracic damage. It can also result from a partial blockage of airway or lungs during a normal ascent from depth.

Gas embolism may take several different forms, depending on where the damage occurs and where the gas has gone. Arterial Gas Embolism (AGE) happens when gas enters the arterial circulation, possibly as a result of a pulmonary barotrauma (eg, a pneumothorax from DCI bubbles bypassing the lung filters, perhaps via a PFO). Damage can occur to vessel linings as the bubbles pass through, causing leakage or inflammation. This can then cause clotting that may itself lead to neurological symptoms. Some bubbles may even be large enough to block circulation, cutting the flow of blood to a vital organ (brain, heart, liver, spleen, kidneys) and further damage may quickly occur. Where the brain is affected, dizziness, uncoordination, paralysis, unconsciousness and even death can rapidly occur. Treatment is by rapid repressurisation (never in the water), and the casualty must be transported in a prone position and given pure oxygen. Artificial respiration and CPR may be required.

Many pneumothoracic injuries need not be chamber treated. Pneumothorax means simply "gas in the chest", and some physical gas pooling can be drained, and oxygen used for surface treatment at atmospheric pressure. Emphysema, a form of pneumothoracic injury which refers to air in tissues, is usually as a result of gas physically escaping into the body due to lung rupture. Mediastinal emphysema is caused by gas escaping into the mediastinum, the space between the lungs and behind the sternum. Symptoms are breathing difficulties, chest pain, and even collapse if pressure on the heart and chest blood vessels becomes too great. Where gas migrates up into the neck tissues, subcutaneous emphysema may result. Subcutaneous means "under the skin", and symptoms include swelling of the affected area, "crackling" skin, breathing difficulties, voice change and difficulty in swallowing.

Major pneumothoracic injuries during ascent can result in the total or partial collapse of one lung when gas enters the pleural cavity. This can lead in turn to respiratory or circulatory difficulties, and possibly death. Symptoms of major pneumothorax include chest pain and reduced chest movement, breathing difficulties, shock, cyanosis and a tendency to lean towards the injured side.

Managing an incident

The key to a diver surviving one of the incidents above lies as much in the efficient management of the response to the incident as in the treatment given. Initial reactions to an emergency differ very much in individuals. Some react positively and can organise themselves and others, well, others simply freeze when things start to go wrong.

Do not allow people to run around in a disorganised fashion. Appoint someone within the group to take charge (it is not a bad idea to do this long before any incidents ever arise) and make sure that they are in charge. Democracy takes second place in emergency reaction.

Split the team into those taking care of the casualty, who should be medically qualified, and those organising the dive area. If at sea, then while the casualty is being brought aboard, make sure others are getting equipment stowed and the boat ready to leave the site. Get someone who knows familiar with the procedure to contact the coastguard and the recompression chamber, and brief them on the patient's real or suspected injuries. Make sure the authorities know which route you will be taking to shore

Communicate with the rescue services on a regular basis, with updates on your position and the state of the casualty. If a helicopter evacuation is planned, make sure someone goes with the casualty, and make sure they are fully briefed on the dive profile, the incident, and the casualty's medical background (where known). They should also have the casualty's name and address, and if possible the name of the next of kin and the casualty's doctor. If no-one can go, make sure all that information is written down and pinned to the casualty, ideally in a waterproof bag.

Keep non-essential personnel away from the casualty. Make sure all other team members are safely on board before leaving the site. If you can, give them something to do to keep morale up, especially if the casualty is in a bad way, and brief them regularly on what is happening. The group controller is responsible for the whole group, not just the casualty. There is always the possibility of others in the group going into shock.

If the accident is due to equipment malfunction, keep the casualty's equipment together, as it was when taken off the diver, and do not allow anyone to touch it. Hand it over to a proper authority when requested, and make sure they know how to handle it, and how to store it. If they obviously do not, try to find someone who does. Request that they bring a member of the local police dive team if necessary. Keep a written record of gas remaining, and any obvious damage that may be visible.

When all is over, try and contact each member of the group in turn, both to let them know what has happened, and to find out any further information that may be required. If the accident has been fatal, all information that may be available should be presented to the coroner, and that will probably be the job of the incident controller.

At best, all will be quickly resolved without further injury, and all will learn from the experience. At worst, you will have done your best in a bad situation, and will be able to pass on the lessons learned to others, in an effort to make sure it doesn't happen again.

CHAPTER EIGHT

Technology

THIS CHAPTER deals with some of the more advanced equipment that may be used by the technical diver. It looks also at the way in which self-contained diving is heading, towards the use of in-water communications integrated with respiratory / buoyancy equipment to form a complete life-support system that not only supplies the diver with breathing gas and buoyancy, but presents it to them in the form of a head-up display, and allows them to communicate voice and data to other divers in the water, or directly to the surface.

It would be wrong to regard this as a look into the future. Many of the component parts of this system already exist, and others are under development. In all probability, such systems will be in regular use within a few months of publication of this book. Most of them will spill over into recreational diving within a very short space of time.

Full-face masks

A full-face mask is a mask that covers not only the diver's eyes and nose, but the entire face from forehead to chin, and which incorporates a regulator into its structure. These are also called band masks, and differ from diving helmets in that the mask forms a seal only round the face, leaving the rest of the head wet. A helmet incorporates a neck seal, keeping the entire head dry. So far, helmets have not made a penetration into the technical diving scene, though full face masks have.

Why use full-face masks? There are several reasons. The first is that they provide the facility for voice communications, it being possible to build a microphone as well as a regulator into the mask. Some microphones are set in front of the mouth, and resonate from direct speech, others use a "bone-conduction" method, where they transmit the vibrations of sound passing through the bones of the head, and where the mouthpiece of the mask is used only to allow the words to be formed and uttered. The signal produced is transmitted to the surface or other divers by various means .

Full-face masks keep the face warmer on long, cold-water exposures, though they can also give a feeling of claustrophobia, for few of the makes currently available give as full a field of vision as the traditional recreational 'half-mask'. They also allow protection for eyes and skin in polluted water.

They provide a real additional benefit to the technical diver on high-oxygen exposures, where the potential for oxygen convulsions exists. If a diver does convulse while wearing a full-face mask, the chance of death by

Top: AGA full face mask. Above: EXO-26 band mask.

drowning is reduced considerably, there being no mouthpiece to spit out or bite through.

Full-face masks generally come in two internal sections, the upper section, which contains the visual lens, and the lower oral-nasal section which covers the mouth and nose. The regulator/s fit through the front or side of the latter, and the snug fit of the mask against the skin allows enough negative internal pressure on inhalation to trigger the demand mechanism of the valve. Because, in most masks, there is no mouthpiece to clench between the teeth, there is less strain on the diver's jaw, and speech is possible.

Nose-clearing is achieved either by pinching the nasal section of a mask or, with some makes, by an integral pinching device, a little like a complicated clothes-peg.

Some masks, like most of the Kirby-Morgan band masks and the Aquadyne DM 5 and 6 series, are really for commercial use, providing a heavy-duty mask that incorporates a separate air supply for umbilical connection, and are not particularly suitable for advanced recreational purposes, being heavy and none too comfortable to swim in. Those suitable for technical diving use are the lighter-weight masks and include the AGA/InterSpiro Divator, the Dräger Modulo 600 and the Kirby-Morgan EXO-26, a lighter-weight version of the commercial series. All of these contain very high-quality regulators, whose performance is entirely suitable for the range of depths, gases and tasks undertaken in technical diving.

They seal by means of a double-seal that runs around forehead, cheeks and jaw, and are held in place by an "octopus" harness with five or more straps to keep the mask close to the head. The mask usually fits over the top of the diver's hood, so if this is a dry-hood, some way of venting off any excess gas that may escape from the mask into the hood may be advisable.

For self-contained use, masks which provide a positive gas flow should be used only in special circumstances. Gas consumption can be enormous, and these only have an advantage in very polluted water, where water ingress is to be avoided at all costs, or in surface-supplied pure oxygen decompression, where it may be necessary *in extremis* to maintain a gas supply gas to a convulsing or unconscious diver. Otherwise, it's a good way of wasting gas. Positive flow is a commercial trick, which helps maintain the oral-nasal cavity clear of CO_2 build-up, and continually flushes water from the upper mask. It is more suited to surface-supplied systems.

In advanced sport diving, the diver should be more in control of his/her environment and diving practice than the average commercial diver, and should be able both to maintain a steady breathing rhythm, and never to approach gas toxicity situations. The technical diver uses the mask to provide diver communication, and to allow an additional margin of safety during oxygen decompressions. It is a tool that is used where applicable, not a tool in which every feature it offers is essential to the task in hand.

Disadvantages of a full-face mask include the potential for CO_2 build up in the oral-nasal cavity, so a steady breathing rhythm is even more important when they are used than with a regulator. With a full-face mask, make sure your breathing is deep and regular, and NEVER attempt to skip-breathe. Such masks do sometimes make the diver feel too isolated from the environment, and demand an extra awareness from the diver as a result.

One major disadvantage of many full-face masks is their lack of redundancy, and the difficulties posed where gas switches are required. Most such masks have a built-in second stage, which offers all the potential for malfunction that any other similar second stage has (inverted exhaust diaphragm, mechanical malfunction, free-flow, etc). While many have the facility for an emergency gas supply, this is usually a free-flow system which would be entirely unsuitable for overhead environments, for example. Some offer no additional supply, and all gas changes have to be done either by a switch bar or by low-pressure snap-connectors. In the latter case, a malfunctioning regulator would involve the diver placing himself at greater risk and higher stress by having to remove the whole mask (effectively blinding himself), finding the bail-out regulator, finding a spare mask and fitting it and clearing it underwater and then making for home. Not a happy situation to be in.

At the time of writing, no one mask offers the potential for full redundancy, where either two second stages can be worn or the second stage can actually be replaced underwater, though there are some under development.

Where rebreathers are used in conjunction with a full-face mask, the bail-out system should be fed straight into the mask, allowing an instant switch in case of rebreather failure.

Maintenance of full-face masks

Maintenance of full-face masks should be a little more thorough than most divers allow for on half-masks. To avoid unhealthy fungal build-up, masks should be cleaned with a suitable detergent and an occasional swill in a mild or dilute disinfectant, the latter being of even more importance when the mask is being used by more than one diver.

The mask should be regularly inspected for deterioration of seals, and it should be stored in a cool dry place. Points requiring lubrication (O-rings, levers, valve assemblies) should only be lubricated with the appropriate lubricant – ie, use oxygen compatible grease where high oxygen mixtures are being used. The communications system should be regularly checked for salt-water damage or material deterioration, and should always be checked on the surface prior to a dive.

Pressure connectors and gas switches

Where full-face masks are being used on occasions that also demand gas switches, but where the facility to change regulators does not exist, provision must be made for a safe way of doing this. There are two main ways in which this can be done in the water by the diver, without requiring an umbilical link to the surface. These are by use of a gas switch bar or by low-pressure snap connectors.

Gas switch bar

This is a bar with multiple inlets and a single or dual outlet that allows various cylinders containing a variety of gas mixes to be used with one or two regulators. By turning levers, or opening valves, the used cylinder can be isolated and a fresh one with an appropriate mix can be accessed. The problem with gas switch bars is an undue dependence on a single second stage, introducing the potential of system failure through a lack of redundancy, and where leakage from a partially-open valve might dilute the breathing gas to an inappropriate mix for the depth of the diver or the stage of the dive.

Low-pressure connectors

These in-line snap-connectors allow low pressure hoses to be connected underwater by the diver, reducing the potential for gas contamination or dilution. They do require more in the way of manual dexterity, and may not be appropriate in certain situations, other than as a back-up device. They allow a single second stage to be used with a variety of first stages, or a variety of second stages to be used with a gas switch bar to allow a degree of redundancy in a gas switch system.

Low pressure connectors can also be fitted to other items of gas equipment, such as inflation hoses, airlifts and the like, which helps reduce the number of hosed accessories the diver may need to carry, or which allows additional items of redundancy to be worn where required. A single spare low-pressure connector can service several items of equipment (eg, air tools, airlifts) if none are essential life-support systems.

Communications systems

A communications system can be as simple as hand signals or tugs on a rope, or as complex as multi-way voice communication using de-scramblers to reduce the distortion caused by pressure changes on the larynx, or by using gas mixtures with a molecular structure different to that of air.

Even with the latter, diver communication should be more than just word-of-mouth. An ideal communication system should provide the facility for diver positioning, so that a supervisor or marshal on the surface can say they know exactly where a diver is at any one time – not simply ' somewhere at the end of this rope/umbilical/cable.' In these days of computer-driven technology, it is possible to envisage a system that transmits not only speech, but allows that signal to be located in real time on a three-dimensional image of the dive site, shown on the screen of a portable computer at the surface, together with data on the diver's breathing patterns, gas use, depth, time, and so on. At the moment, facilities exist for part of this system on the latest generation of rebreathers, but the full 3-D location system is not too far off.

Avoiding rope and hand signals, which are well covered elsewhere and which can be developed and adapted on the day to suit simple diver-to-diver and diver-to-surface communications, we will regard communications here as being a method by which one diver speaks to another or transmits hard and occasionally complex data via a definite link. Though hand signals can be as complex as, for example, deaf-and-dumb sign language (at some learning obligation to the diver) they still demand a close visual contact, and are useful as a means of surface communication only with a visual link. Rope signals can easily be misinterpreted, and umbilicals of any sort are prone to snag. A free-swimming diver may not be in direct visual contact with a partner, possibly through conditions of darkness or reduced visibility. He is not likely to have a direct umbilical link to the surface.

Currently, most modern diver communications centre on through-water transmissions of one sort of another. Most carry speech in conjunction with a full-face mask and either a direct microphone or a bone-conducting system. In the latter, the microphone can also be used as the speaker if required, though at the expense of one-way-at-a-time transmission. The actual transmitter/receiver is usually mounted on the diver's waist or back, and forms a fairly bulky item that reduces streamlining and adds additional weight, though this can be reduced by removing lead from the weightbelt. An in-line waterproof connector allows the full-face mask to be removed from the communications system.

These systems vary in range from a few dozen metres to over 3 kilometres, though transmission is affected by thermoclines and haloclines present in the surrounding water, which reflect radio-waves. Dropping a receiver from the surface to the diver's depth and transmitting horizontally may increase the strength of the signal reception. Transmission itself can be voice-activated or PTT (push-to-talk), depending on the degree of sophistication of the unit, and whether or not it is convenient to manually operate the transmitter.

Communications system: Top – diver unit and (above) surface unit.

Such communications systems are of great use where data collection is required, as speech from the diver can be recorded and transcribed later, allowing greater use to be made of observational data than were the diver to record it manually. They also allow diver-to-diver communication, a real asset where more complex instructions may have to be passed underwater. They also have a place in diver instruction, and where a solo diver needs to have a communication link with the surface.

Scooters

Many technical divers increasingly use underwater diver propulsion vehicles (DPV's) to increase their range or make more effective use of their dive time. Though divers have been experimenting with DPVs for decades, in military and scientific circles, their use by technical divers has developed via the cave diving community. Cave divers in North America and France, where underground passages are large and clear enough to allow use of such vehicles, have developed their expertise in the techniques of DPV driving to a fine art.

Several commercial makes of DPV have come and gone from the market in recent years, including the once-popular Farallon and Tekna range. Favourites among technical divers in the early 1990's are the Aquazepps of Germany, with DiveRite of Florida about to enter the lists with a model similar to the Aquazepp-LS.

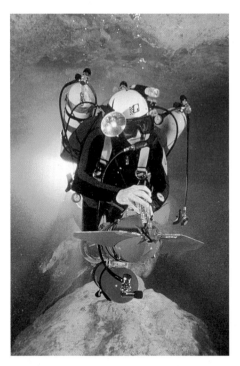

A DPV in use by a technical diver.

Different models of DPV either drag the diver along behind or allow him/her to straddle the unit, squatting astride a T-bar like a horse or motor cycle, with the diver steering the device by body and fin control.

Those on which the diver sits are fitted with some kind of seat, either a T-bar or a modified bicycle-type seat which allows the diver to slide their legs below the bar and ride securely on the vehicle. Depending on just how much weight and mass the DPV is expected to propel through the water, some modifications may be necessary to the bar that comes with the DPV to make it strong enough to cope.

You may also need to make some modifications to your own diving equipment. Gauges that hang down loose can easily be sucked into the propeller to result in a broken driveshaft and a mashed gauge. The complications caused by either of these happening are obvious. Make sure all your contents gauges, regulators, straps and danglies are secured to your person, and offer no opportunity for entanglement in the propeller. A mesh guard on the propeller may be a useful modification, although it may also reduce the motive power of the unit.

Where a number of stage cylinders are worn or carried, the distribution of weight becomes crucial. An unskilled driver may find it impossible to steer in a straight line horizontally with triple cylinders, or even a heavy twinset, without making some adjustment to the vehicle's trim. In some cases, where stage cylinders are actually strapped to the DPV itself, an additional buoyancy compensator may be fitted to the unit to allow a degree of vehicular buoyancy control. The inflation for this BC should be run from the stage cylinders on the DPV.

Divers should always be attached to the DPV by a line with a quick-release clip. This reduces the chance of losing a DPV in deep water if you let go and the unit is negatively buoyant. Another useful addition is a "Dead Man's Throttle", which when released cuts power to the engine. This further reduces the chance of loss by one of the beasts roaring off on its own. It also means that if something does happen to you – like a collision with a piece of wreck or a cave roof knocking you out – then you will not be towed away unconscious from the dive site. In the latter case, a unit with slight positive buoyancy may be better than a negative one. It is worth considering using a helmet when riding a DPV – collisions are more common than you might think, and a helmet may make all the difference.

When a pull-unit is being used, the diver should be attached securely to the DPV by a tow strap from the scooter to a D-ring on their diving harness. Properly adjusted, this reduces strain on the diver's arms, and allows one hand to be taken off the DPV to do other tasks. It also allows the DPV to be steered with the hands rather than the fins, a slight tug with either hand being all that is needed to change direction.

Overhead environments of any sort should be avoided until the diver is very proficient with a DPV in open water. Collisions with walls, roofs and floors are all inevitable with an inexperienced operator, and the resulting sediment disturbance can quickly reduce visibility to zero.

Sediments are a major problem where scooter wash is concerned. Avoid pointing the propeller at silt or sediments when starting up – rise a metre or so above the bottom first, and settle your trim. Stay away from banks of sediment in wrecks or caves, and clear of the bottom in open water – you can

do a lot of environmental damage without realising it. If you are passing through any confined areas or low passages, get off the scooter and swim it – again, practice this first in open water.

Remember also, if you are penetrating into any type of overhead environment on a scooter, that you use very much less breathing gas on a DPV. If it fails when you are deep inside, will you still have enough gas left to get out and reach the surface safely? It is best to limit scooter dives to open water, unless you are extremely experienced in the special problems posed by penetrating into overhead environments, and are trained accordingly.

DPV's do offer many advantages. The obvious ones are that the diver can cover more ground than by free-swimming and use less gas. This is as appropriate at 50 metres as at 20, but it can be very easy to forget depth rules when on a scooter, and do short dips below the target depth. Dive planning is every bit as essential when using a scooter, and the laws of nature cover DPV drivers every bit as much as free-swimmers. Keep within your dive plan and your gas and depth limitations,

DPV's come with different power outputs, and thus different ranges. Dive plans should be made that allow the scooter to work within its known range, and recovery procedures should plan to get it on your boat without damaging either the scooter or the boat. A small winch is ideal.

Above left: A DPV tow strap. Above right: An Aquazepp scooter with stage cylinders fixed beneath for an extended technical dive.

Planning a scooter dive

There are a few new equipment checks that need to be added to your list when planning a dive using DPV's. They are, in no particular order:

1   Is the battery freshly-charged?
2   Are all DPV clips and plugs secure?
3   Am I clipped to the DPV?
4   Can I reach all my gauges and regulators easily?
5   Are my gauges, hoses and other equipment safely secure?
6   Is my buoyancy adequate and correct?
7   Can I swim back from where I am going?

With DPV's, as with any other battery-operated diving device, make sure you charge the batteries properly after every dive. Do not leave the unit in a low or uncharged state for long -this may seriously damage the batteries, and a battery stack for a DPV is considerably more expensive than that for a torch.

Things that limit the range offered by your batteries are: bad charging practices; running under a consistent heavy load; carrying additional equipment (stage tanks, cameras, etc), towing another diver; or running a DPV with an onboard light on. Some makes of DPV have an integral light unit that can easily be disconnected to reduce power drain. Make relevant adjustments accordingly.

Computers

Computers in a variety of forms are becoming more and more a part of diving. Decompression computers evolved from decompression meters in the late 1970's, and by the late 1980's were visible in one shape or size on the arm of almost every diver.

The only real variation, apart from shape and colour, was the degree of sophistication offered by the unit, and the algorithm on which it based its calculations (see Chapter 4). The new generation of dive computers from Oceanic, Seiko, Uwatec, Orca and Suunto can interface with a home computer, to allow dives to be downloaded into the memory of a software logbook, and even allow a degree of forward planning on the screen. As these computers become more proficient and complex, this interface facility will undoubtedly increase, offering home users the same sort of planning facility for customised gas mixtures that diving computer experts now offer at a price.

Various early ventures into this market provide interactive programmes which allow the user to find an appropriate gas mix for a dive, to ascertain what steps need to be taken to manufacture that mix, and to generate an appropriate set of decompression tables for use with that mix, taking into account any other gas changes that may be available during the dive. Such very sophisticated programmes should only be used in their advanced stages by divers with a considerable understanding of the problems of physiology and exposure, but in their simpler versions they provide a technical diver with a considerable degree of planning advantage for multi-pro-

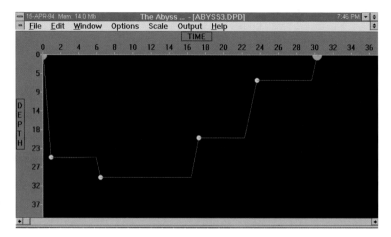

A dive-planner screen display.

file nitrox or air dives. These programmes usually allow the user to programme a percentage safety factor into the tables – very useful if the diver knows that they are less fit than they ought to be, or that conditions will be more strenuous than normal. The most sophisticated programmes carry the additional facility in advanced versions for computing mixed gas decompressions on trimix or heliox, in open and closed circuit systems.

It must be remembered that such programmes are simply generating a mathematical response to a mathematical programme – profiles generated by such systems have not been fully field-tested, and work on mathematically-inspired "ought to be OK" principle. This does not necessarily mean they are unsafe, simply that they should be used, like any dive computer, with due caution, and ideally with a full understanding of the physiological implications and inhibiting factors of the particular dive profile to be undertaken.

Head-up displays

Developments in visual display of the data have complemented the development of diving-related computer systems. Within a few years, most divers will see their dive data (depth, time, decompression information, etc) displayed in front of their eyes, in a "head-up" format similar to those used by military pilots in helicopters and fighter planes. These tiny display units will fasten to the side of the diver's mask or helmet, and will remove much of the need constantly to be glancing at the instrument panel on the arm. With the increasing sophistication of computer monitoring systems, it will be soon possible to add data on the diver's personal state of health – body temperature, pulse rate and so on – perhaps even with the addition of personal doppler monitoring.

All this can provide an enormous degree of environmental cushioning. A good diver will still need to be aware of his environment, and of the skills required to survive when the electronics go wrong, or get beyond remote control. But, like a good photographer when faced with sophisticated camera equipment, or a racing driver with a more sophisticated car, it is the eye behind the camera, or the hand on the wheel, that makes the final difference. Never imagine you are good simply because you own the equipment. It's knowing how to use it properly that counts.

Portable recompression chambers

In remote locations, where recompression facilities are few and far between, thought should be given to the use of appropriate types of recompression therapy. There are essentially three choices.
1   Don't do any diving, or keep it very shallow with no provocative exposures. But one can argue that any exposure is provocative, and injuries requiring recompression therapy can occur in 20 metres or less of water.
2   Only dive where established recompression facilities are available. Lists of recompression chambers are readily available, though may on occasion be inaccurate or out-of-date. Always check whether a recompression chamber is operational, and what its capabilities are, before committing yourself to a provocative diving programme in a remote area.
3   Use in-water recompression (see Chapter 7). In warm protected water, with a full-face mask and a plentiful supply of therapy gas, that may be appropriate, though few authorities recommend it. It can produce problems where secondary treatment is required, or where symptoms

The SOS Hyperlite portable recompression chamber.

worsen. The main problem is that there is no way to transport the diver, once treatment is underway, to a place with better treatment facilities.

4   Portable recompression chambers. These are probably the best option, if a suitable one can be found. Unfortunately most of the current "portable" chambers require a large trailer, a small crane, and either a ship, a large helicopter or decent sized lorry to move them about. Some good dive boats may have one on board, or the facilities to ship one, and for a serious programme of deep diving it may be worth hiring one of these. Few really portable chambers exist. At the time of writing, probably the best of these is the SOS Hyperlite, a collapsible, seamless Kevlar tube that can be erected in minutes and carried, with the casualty, by four adults. It can be pressurised to 3 bar and therapeutic oxygen fed via a BIBS system to the patient inside. It fits on to or into most larger therapeutic chambers, so a patient can be transported under pressure for some distance (assuming a portable supply of oxygen) to a better equipped chamber somewhere else. Simple bends cases can be fully treated to resolution on site.

Unfortunately, such chambers are one-person chambers, and do not allow medical attention where the casualty is exhibiting other symptoms, and so are limited in their application. Plans for a two-man chamber, where additional treatment can be given, are still on the drawing board through lack of funding.

There is no easy answer to remote-location high-exposure diving. Like high-exposure mountaineering, or remote-location travel, the risks must be assessed and the divers must decide for themselves whether the rewards are worth the dangers. That does not mean it should not be done. It simply means that the onus is again on the divers, not the system, to plan their own futures. If they are well-trained, well-equipped and prepared, their motivation is genuine, and they understand the conditions, then such diving should not be inappropriate.

Habitats

We are not talking here about habitats of the "SEALAB" type, but about decompression habitats that allow divers some respite from the elements during long decompressions. They vary from a simple "wet-bell" to a more complex, diver-winchable dry chamber in which the diver can actually leave the water while decompressing.

The use of such systems, developed from commercial operations, where divers working at depth were taken up and down in a diving bell, either in a gas or water atmosphere depending on the degree of exposure of the dive. Obviously the safe use of such a system depends on a well-trained and well-equipped surface support crew, and the whole operation is too expensive by far to consider using on an average recreational dive.

As technical diving exposures became longer and deeper, notably in US cave diving, technical divers started to consider the use of habitat-like structures in which they could decompress in greater comfort and a more controlled environment. On deep marine dives, shark cages were used as decompression cages, where protection from teeth became a secondary consideration, and somewhere more comfortable to decompress came first. Decompression gas could be staged therein, or fed down from the surface, the divers could be monitored, could relax more, and if problems arose they could be more easily contained.

In caves, the problems of excessive buoyancy of a gas-filled habitat were solved by simply finding a bit of flat roof at the appropriate depth, and placing the habitat below that, up against the rock. Old circular cattle-troughs (" habi-troughs") are a favourite – stable, deep enough to get the diver's head out of the water, and large enough to accommodate pairs of divers at a time. To avoid the problem of CO_2 and nitrogen build-up, diver's continue to breathe through their regulators, or from oro-nasal masks on the end of surface-fed umbilicals. They offer the chance to switch to a full-face mask in an air environment when pure oxygen decompressions are to be made above 6 metres. Short bursts of conversation are possible, and, by being at least partially out of the water, thermal exposure is reduced. Some divers experiment with tape and rope slings, as mini-trapezes hung below the

Divers decompressing in an underwater decompression habitat.

A multi-person habitat.

chambers. Others simply maintain positive buoyancy and float on the "underwater water-surface".

Such decompression habitats only work where there is a roof to place them under that is capable of supporting the positive buoyancy exerted by the unit. These habitats work on the same physical principal as a lifting bag; try the same concept in a wreck, or other less structurally sound site, and you may find both you and the habitat heading for the surface.

Closed decompression habitats in open water are more difficult to arrange. In many cases, sticking to the wet-bell or cage principle is probably more appropriate. If it is preferable to have some degree of airspace to support the diver, then due attention must be paid to providing a source of negative buoyancy to counteract the lift of the chamber section. If a secure enough source of weight can be found, then a chamber of some description can be hung above it. A constant-volume chamber is better, otherwise as it ascends between stops, the volume of gas inside expands, increasing the lift and counteracting the weight below.

Several methods exist which enable the diver to operate the raising and lowering of the habitat. The simplest is by using climbing-style ascenders (Jumars) to winch a small habitat higher in the water. Alternatively, a system of pulleys can be used to raise or lower the habitat. Mobile habitats of this nature were used very successfully on the 1987 Wakulla Project by cave divers exploring North Florida's Wakulla Springs. Open circuit dives at depths of 100 metres or so for long bottom times meant that decompressions were several hours long, and the degree of exposure was effectively controlled by the use of this multi-person habitat

Postscript

*"The real explorer is the one who reaches the summit and comes back.
The one who reaches the summit and doesn't come back is a failure."*

Lord Hunt, Leader,
1953 British Everest Expedition

AS STATED so many times within, what you do underwater should be up to you. If you have read this far, you should understand the need for due respect for the underwater environment, the need for proper and appropriate training, and for proper and appropriate equipment. The only additional ingredient for the technical diving recipe is you.

Why do you want to do it? Re-read the introduction and decide for yourself whether you have the aptitude and experience to proceed from recreational diving to technical diving. NO-ONE can or should make the choice for you other than yourself. We go diving for pleasure, not to scare ourselves witless, or to endanger our minds and bodies beyond what we consider our acceptable limits. We have a responsibility not only to ourselves, but to our families and loved ones, and we need to make sure that we, and they, understand and appreciate all the risks involved. And where others are involved, the risks need to be as few as possible. You are not the one who will organise your funeral, or weep at your grave.

There is another little acronym for use in technical diving: **AKTEE.**

- **A** is for **ATTITUDE** : Why are you doing this?
- **K** is for **KNOWLEDGE** : Without knowledge, you have no options.
- **T** is for **TRAINING** : Make skills second nature – "muscle memory".
- **E** is for **EQUIPMENT** : The right tools for the job.
- **E** is also for **EXPERIENCE** : This takes time – there are few shortcuts.

No diving is safe, all diving carries risks. Technical diving, properly done, is all about safe exploration beyond the recreational range. It carries a higher potential for risk, but it does not need to be dangerous unless you make it so. Stay safe, stay warm, plan well, and carry enough gas.

References

OTHER primary works on the subject of technical diving, or on advanced diving techniques, are listed below. The list is by no means exhaustive, and the reader is reminded that this is not a training manual, and nor are many of the books in this list. Each of the books below contains further references, and the books listed here are ones I would personally recommend as taking you a stage further in your studies.

There is no substitute for proper training, other than the considerable risks incurred by the gaining of appropriate experience without training, and so following the list of books is a list of organisations supplying that training. At the end of the reference section is a conversions table, supplying metric to imperial (and vice versa) diving measurements of distance, volume and capacity. There are no decompression tables given for air, nitrox, trimix or heliox, as these are available in the relevant training manuals, though I would recommend from personal experience the use of the Bühlmann or DCIEM tables for air or nitrox EADs, and one of the many versions of the DCAP programme, or a series of tables based on an appropriate gas algorithm, for use with gas mixtures other than air or nitrox.

Books

Nitrox Manual. R. Palmer. Technical Diving International (Europe), 1994.
The Essentials of Deeper Sport Diving. John Lippmann. Aqua Quest Publications, 1992. ISBN 0 9623389 3 1
Deep Diving. Bret Gilliam et al. Watersports Publishing, 1992. ISBN 0-922769-30-0
Mixed Gas. Bret Gilliam and Tom Mount. Watersports Publishing, 1992. ISBN 0-922769-41-9
IANTD Nitrox Manual. International Association of Technical and Nitrox Divers, 1993.
IANTD (UK) Nitrox Manual. Rob Palmer and Kevin Gurr. International Association of Nitrox and Technical Divers, (UK) 1993.
The Use and Application of Enriched Air Mixtures. Ed Betts. American Nitrox Divers Inc, 1992
Cave Diving. (Balcombe, Cordingley, Palmer and Stevenson, editors) Castle Cary Press, 1990. ISBN 0-905903-14-5
NSS-CDS Cave Diving Manual. Eds. Prosser. J. and Grey H.V. PO Box 950, Blandford, Florida 3208-0950 USA, 1992
Drysuit Diving. Barsky, Long and Stinton. Watersports Publications, 1992. ISBN 0-922-769-36-2
Stress and Performance in Diving. Bacharach and Egstrom. Best Publishing Co, 1987

The DAN Emergency Handbook. Lippmann and Buggs. JL Publications, 1989

US Navy Diving Manual (Vol 1 – Air). NAVSEA., Best Publishing Co, 1991

US Navy Diving Manual (Mixed Gas). NAVSEA, Best Publishing Co, 1992

Deeper Into Diving. John Lippman. JL Publications,1990

Advanced Wreck Diving Guide. Gary Gentile. Cornell Maritime Press, 1988

Ultimate Wreck Diving Guide. Gary Gentile. 1992

NOAA Diving Manual. James Millar (Ed). US Government Printing Office.

Diving and Subaquatic Medicine. Edmonds, Lowery and Pennegather. Best Publishing Co, 1983

The Physician's Guide to Diving Medicine. Shilling, Carlston and Mathias. Plenum Press, 1984

Physiology and Medicine of Diving. Bennett P. and Elliott D. 4th Edition 1993. W.B.Saunders & Co, Ltd, London, 1993. ISBN 0-7020-1589-X

Dive Computers. Loyst, Huggins and Steidley. Watersports Publishing Inc, 1991

Cold Weather and Under Ice Scuba Diving, NAUI/NDA Technical Publication No.4. Lee Somers. NAUI 1973

Code of Practice for Scientific Diving. Nic Fleming and Michael Max, Eds. UNESCO Technical Papers in Marine Science No 53. UNESCO, 1988. ISBN 0503-4299

Workshop on Enriched Air Nitrox Diving. Hamilton, Crosson and Hulbert, Eds. National Undersea Research Program Report 89-1. NOAA 1989

Periodicals

Diver Magazine
Editorial Address: 55 High Street, Teddington, Middlesex TW11 8HA (tel. 081-943 4288, fax 081-943 4312).

Sea Technology
Compass Publications Inc, Suite 1000, 1117 NW 19th St, Arlington, VA 22209, USA (tel. 703-524-3136, fax 703-841-0852). Monthly magazine looking at advances in all marine and underwater technology.

Training organisations

International Association of Nitrox and Technical Divers (UK) Limited
42 Marsh Road, Thatcham, Berkshire RG13 4DR, UK.
Courses in nitrox, trimix, rebreathers, deep diving and overhead environment diving.

International Association of Nitrox and Technical Divers
1545 NE 104th St., Miami Shores, Florida Fl33138, USA.
Courses in nitrox, trimix, rebreathers, deep diving, overhead environments, cave diving.

International Association of Nitrox and Technical Divers (Australia)
255 Stanmore Road, Stanmore, NSW 2048, Australia.
All IANTD courses.

American Nitrox Divers Incorporated
UK address: 74 Woodcleft Avenue, Freeport, New York, NY 11520, USA.
Nitrox courses.

Technical Diving International
621 Cuda Lane, Key Largo, Florida, Fl-33037, USA (tel. 305-853-0966; fax 305-852-3908).

Technical Diving (Europe) Ltd
Langlands Business Park, Uffculme, Cullompton, Devon EX15 3DA

NSS Cave Diving Section
PO Box 950, Branford, Florida, Fl-32008-0950, USA.
Cave and cavern diving training courses.

National Association of Cave Divers
PO Box 14492, Gainesville, Florida, Fl 32604, USA.
Cave and cavern diving training courses.

Cave Diving Group
Secretary: 16 Warren Close, Sandhurst, Camberley, Surrey GU17 8EL, UK.
Cave diving training for experienced cavers only. No courses.

Confederation Mondiale des Activities Subaquatiques (World Underwater Federation)
Viale Tiziano 74, 00196 Rome, Italy.

Formulae

Dalton's Law equations

Where   **PPg** = Partial Pressure of a gas
             P   = Absolute Pressure in bar
             Fg   = Fraction of the gas in mixture.

a) To find the partial pressure of a gas at a given depth:

PPg = Fg x P

b) To find the best fraction of oxygen to use in order not to exceed the tolerance dose – (eg, PPO_2 of 1.6 bar):

FO_2 = PPO_2 divided by P

c) To find the maximum oxygen tolerance depth for any gas mix:

P = PPO_2 divided by FO_2
then use   **MOD = D = (P – 1) x 10(metres)**

Equivalent air depth

$$EAD = \frac{(1 - FO_2) \times (D + 10)}{0.79} - 10$$

Depth equations

a) Where   **D** = depth in metres
                 P = Absolute Pressure in bar.

D = (P – 1) x 10

P = D/10 + 1

b) Where   **D** = depth in feet
                 P = Absolute Pressure in ATA

D = (P – 1) x 33

P = D/33 + 1

Nitrox mixing

(Only to be applied by qualified blenders with appropriate equipment – to use otherwise may be life-threatening).

To find O_2 quantity to add to cylinder for nitrox mix :

$$O_2 = \frac{FO_2 - 0.21}{0.79} \text{ x pressure of cylinder}$$

Gas consumption

Where   **T** = time in minutes
            V = Volume in free litres,
            P = Absolute Pressure in bar
            R = Ventilation volume in litres per minute.

$$T = \frac{V}{(P \times R)} \quad \text{and} \quad V = P \times R \times T$$

Volumetric content of a cylinder

Where   **C** = contents in free litres,
            VW = cylinder volume in litres of water
            WP = working pressure in bar.

$$C = VW \times WP$$

CONVERSION FORMULAE

To convert	into	multiply by
ATA	FSW	33.9
	PSI	14.7
bar	ATA	0.986
	PSI	14.5
Cu ft.	Litres	28.32
Cu.metres	Litres	1000
FSW	ATA	0.295
	MSW	0.3048
	PSI	0.445
Litres	Cu.Ft.	0.03531
	Cu.Metres	0.001
MSW	ATA	(0.1) + 1
	FSW	2.307

Index